TALKIN' CHALK

Rebecca West

TALKIN' CHALK

10 TIPS FOR BEGINNING TEACHERS

amba press

My dear hubby, Steve.

Without you, I wouldn't have the capacity to help my fellow teachers. I am forever grateful for your support, guidance and encouragement. You make my world a calmer and funnier place.

Milk.

Eggs.

Coffee.

To my Pickle Princess, Mr Nuggens and Eggy,
you are my world and my treasures. I love you bigger than the sweetest dreams in the night sky, to the moon and back.

For all my Clever Pickles,
I am truly grateful to have been your teacher in this lifetime.
I feel proud to have known and taught you all.

Published in 2023 by Amba Press, Melbourne, Australia
www.ambapress.com.au

© Rebecca West 2023

All rights reserved. No part of this book may be reproduced or transmitted in any form or by any means, electronic or mechanical, including photocopying, recording or by any information storage and retrieval system, without prior permission in writing from the publisher.

Cover design: Tess McCabe
Internal design: Amba Press
Editor: Rica Dearman
Printing: IngramSpark

ISBN: 9781922607485 (pbk)
ISBN: 9781922607492 (ebk)

A catalogue record for this book is available from the National Library of Australia.

Contents

Preface	ix
Accurate, but not verifiable, teacher facts	1
Tip 1 Plan your classroom set-up	5
Tip 2 Know your way around	21
Tip 3 Start your program with skeletons	31
Tip 4 Plan for short-term and long-term organisation	49
Tip 5 Monitor your workload	63
Tip 6 Proactively build relationships	71
Tip 7 Set clear and explicit expectations	79
Tip 8 Persevere and reflect on practice	89
Tip 9 Be kind to the relief teacher	97
Tip 10 Try an additional role	111
Conclusion: It's an evolving career	117
Templates: Sharing is caring	119
About the author	147

Preface

One of my favourite quotes comes from Simon Sinek, someone I draw great inspiration from. He said: "People don't buy what you do; they buy why you do it. And what you do simply proves what you believe." I believe the education system is one of the most important societal constructs. Having this system in place acknowledges that learning is valuable, and we all gain something beneficial from being part of the process. I also know that one system does not work for all. I believe lifelong learning is important for all humankind, and that is why I am proud to be an educator.

If you are a teacher – new or experienced – you will experience consistent changes in the education system. It evolves, as society does, and it is imperative that all educators share their knowledge and insights with one another if we are to maintain a system that provides quality and equitable learning opportunities for all. When I first became a teacher, I relied on advice from colleagues in my immediate team and my supervisor. There was no one else. In my first years as an Assistant Principal, I tried to share my knowledge and advice as best as I could with my teams and across the school, with the minimal resources available at the time. That meant there was a limit to what I could do, who I could reach and how this would support student improvement. It was hard to feel like I was making a sustainable or significant impact.

Now we live in a world where advice and collaboration can be accessed with the click of a button or swipe of a touchscreen. In 2017, I started a YouTube channel to help my students become engaged in learning maths by making videos of maths games using resources they could access at home. I was inspired by flipped learning and tried to incorporate that pedagogy into my classroom. It was highly successful and led to some colleagues suggesting I should also share the teaching perspective with my peers, and I then started another channel for teachers called Talkin' Chalk. On this channel I share tips and resources with the occasional livestream where I get to learn and collaborate with others. The YouTube channel has now generated a following of teachers and it illustrates just how many teachers there are out there who want to work together and share beyond their immediate team or network.

It also highlights that, as educators, we all have something unique to offer. My tips might be different to someone else's or could be perfectly in line with the way another person thinks. The feedback has been highly positive and supportive, so now I'm taking an even further leap and attempting to put my words to paper in the hope that teachers reading this feel supported, valued and possibly gain something beneficial that enhances the way they teach or how their students learn. Ultimately, if I can help teachers as much as possible, then I'm helping more students as well – and our students are always our main priority.

This book is based on my own experiences from almost two decades of teaching and is aimed at those who are new to teaching, but if it appeals to more experienced educators, then I hope you take something useful away from reading it as well. Quality teachers are lifelong learners and will always be willing to try something new – especially if it creates learning opportunities for their students.

My advice is not the be all and end all. Teachers need to become confident enough to trust their own judgement. You will come to know your kids best and what they need to thrive. I'm sharing what has worked for me, hoping it might help others start their journey as a teacher. My hope is that this book enhances your confidence a little and helps you find your way in those first days and weeks of having a class of your very own. Try and take the time to soak up those memories. You will never forget your first class.

Sharing is caring.

Accurate, but not verifiable, teacher facts

Being a teacher is a way of life and consumes our hearts. There are some random things we experience being a teacher:

- When young boys come to you for help with untied, wet shoelaces, remember something very important – that is NOT likely from water! It is rarely from water!

- Chip packets get tougher every year. The kids have already been trying to open them with greasy fingers and your hands will end up just as greasy trying to open them. Be friendly with the canteen staff so they can keep a pair of scissors on hand for cutting those tough packets open. Or keep tissues handy for wiping off the pack.

- Students will call you Mum on average 2,387 times a day. They won't call you Dad, even if you are a dad – you'll still be called Mum. I choose to believe it means they feel safe.

- If you become a teacher before becoming a parent, there will be at least 15 names on your veto list based on kids that stretched your patience or were popularly overused.

- You will experience all sorts of interaction with vomit, snot, urine and poo in your career – sometimes directly on your new favourite jumper. And it's not necessarily going to be from the youngest students. Always have spare clothes.

- No matter how much you train students to cough and sneeze into their elbow, they will do it right in your face, when you least expect it, and your mouth will absolutely be wide open when it happens. Stock up on flu remedies.

- Kids are very honest. Not mean, just brutally honest. If they poke your belly and ask you if you're pregnant, they're not trying to tease you. They're just stating an observation. It works both ways, though – if they tell you that you're beautiful, you can believe they genuinely mean it.

- When a student brings in cupcakes and lolly bags to celebrate their birthday, put them in the staff fridge with a *Do Not Touch!* label and wait till 10 minutes before the last bell to hand them out. They can enjoy a lovely sugar rush after they have finished school for the day. If this isn't possible, then wait till the beginning of lunch break to hand them out and hope they run it out of their system during playtime.

- Avoid a traditional teacher's whistle. The first time you ask a kid to grab your keys you can be guaranteed the first thing they will do is have a nice, sharp, wet blow on that thing for a laugh. The class will giggle and laugh. You will not.

- Do NOT leave your permanent markers anywhere near the whiteboard markers. In fact, don't leave them anywhere near the whiteboard. I'm sure we know that permanent marker comes off when you write over it with a whiteboard marker, but just save yourself the trouble and keep the permanent markers away from the risk.

- It really doesn't matter what grade you teach – all kids love a good scratch 'n' sniff sticker. Always have a good stash of them. Especially now you can get such an assortment of scents like donuts, bacon and coffee! Back in my day, we were lucky to get sweet banana or bubble gum.

- Kids are always picking flowers to gift to their teacher. Have a little glass or pot to keep them in for the day. No gift is too small, and it shows that they are thinking of you.

- Kids will fart. Giggle on the inside, but open a window and keep teaching. The more it's acknowledged, the less you will be able to get on with the lesson. Fragrance diffusers help.
- Being a teacher will make you experience all sorts of emotions, good and bad. It will test you, push you, help you grow and show you some of the best parts of humanity. Kids are awesome, even the tough ones. Never forget it.

Tip 1

Plan your classroom set-up

A classroom will become a 'home away from home' for you and your students. They will grow and develop in that space and will likely spend more time in that room than they will spend in their own lounge room. As a teacher, you won't just spend your teaching time in there, but your mornings, afternoons and evenings as well.

Your main goal in designing and creating a learning environment is ensuring that all students – and teachers – that engage in the classroom are comfortable and develop the confidence to be themselves in that space. Your classroom will be a place for learning, but it can involve a range of emotions and experiences depending on your students. There's a very good chance kids will be happy, scared, embarrassed, angry, unsure, sad and, from time to time, it will be a space where someone wets their pants, farts or vomits on the floor – this is not solely restricted to the students!

Many teachers have spent time in their room sharing lunch, having a celebratory afternoon tea, singing along with music while tidying, reflecting on the day, laughing with their neighbour teacher and sometimes even hiding in the storeroom for a cry. Anything can happen in a classroom; the overall aim is to create a space where great things can happen for anyone who learns there, including you.

Much like your home, your classroom will have visitors. The teacher next door, other students, parents, the principal and sometimes even the head honchos of your system. It's worthwhile to remember your room is one of the most important places in your school. This does not mean there is an expectation for your classroom to be picture-perfect, but it should be very clear that learning and teaching occurs in that space and that the students are significant contributors to the learning processes within it.

Resources and storage

> "The trouble with, 'A place for everything, and everything in its place' is that there's always more everything than places."
>
> – Robert Brault

Teachers are constant collectors. Collectors of resources, materials, craft supplies, stickers, stamps, pencils, beanbags, pillows, books, games, movies, posters and I'm sure there's a kitchen sink in some teacher's storeroom somewhere, literally. Before online resources were so readily available, many teacher storerooms were packed to the rafters with programs, textbooks, blackline masters and syllabus documents. Now, with a simple search and click, you can access all of that in the blink of an eye, and yet, many teacher storerooms are still full!

Why? Well, teachers seem to be a very special type of recycler. We see the value in the most random things. Egg cartons as paint holders, takeaway food containers to store card games, sauce containers to hold counters and dice, cube storage for fancy dress costumes, pocket wall hangers to store student notes and reminders... the list is endless! It's easy to get swept up in the great things we find, and sometimes we don't focus on the logistics of using many things. Some schools have great resources, and others not so much so. Some schools won't have vast storage for individual teachers – some classrooms don't have a storeroom at all!

It's important to plan specifically for resources that you keep. What will you keep it for and why is it a worthwhile resource to store?

I don't believe you need to aspire to have what many refer to as an 'Instagram Classroom'. However, I do believe it's beneficial to take this approach with storage. It becomes detrimental if you don't have your resources clearly labelled, organised and stored for easy access. You risk having items lost, damaged or worse – unused! The same applies to your digital resources, online and on hard drive. Keep things organised in a way that suits you, making it easy to access in years to come. Name digital files specifically, include years and subjects. Label boxes clearly, keeping similar items together.

If you are fortunate to have a storeroom in your classroom, keep some shelves empty in the storeroom (and in the classroom) for school resources. You will likely have things allocated to your classroom such as library books, mathematics resources and reading sets. This will minimise the risk that they become mixed up with your own belongings. Label these shelves or spaces as school resources (or something suitable) and make sure anyone who needs to use things from here know where to return items – I recommend keeping the storeroom a 'teacher only' space. Be mindful of using labels that are easy to remove at the end of the year in case you change classrooms or if you want to re-label at any point. Printed tags with Blu-Tack are a good option. Avoid sticky labels that will leave a mess after removing.

When you use the storeroom to store items of your own, it is beneficial to use shelves at eye level for things that you will readily use across the year, for that class. If you have a stockpile of resources for older or younger students, these are best kept out of easy reach, like on the top or bottom shelves to await another year. If you have lots of books and deep shelves, you can double up by putting books you won't use behind books you will use regularly. It pays to invest in some magazine-style book boxes to protect the longevity of your books. Many children's picture books and novels have flimsy spines and cannot last years of being wedged next to each other. Ensure these books are clearly labelled, as you never know when they might be appropriate for your current class. Make sure your name is in those books, as these will often become mixed up with library books, school supplies or even lost in other classrooms if colleagues are sharing books.

When it comes to selecting storage boxes, it really is worth investing in hard plastic boxes that are stackable, and set yourself a limit. The more boxes you buy, the more likely you will hoard items that don't get used. For example, label one box as 'celebrations' and keep this for items for Easter, Christmas, etc. Each year, see what you use, and if there is space, you can put more in it. If you didn't use anything, then evaluate if the items are worth keeping.

Here is a storeroom example. Let's imagine that you are teaching a Year 6 class and have a storeroom with two sets of shelves. You walk in and have shelves to your left and shelves to your right. Let's also imagine you have collected lots of resources suitable for K-2 and likely won't use them this year. Use the middle shelf for the resources you will use for this class and then use the bottom shelf for things saved for younger classes and top shelf for school-allocated resources. This makes it easy to access relevant materials, easy to find other resources when needed and saves your back in the process.

If you need to store items in your home, using clear labels will make it easier when you need to rotate resources between home and school. It took me a long time to get to a place where I no longer have any school resources being stored in my home. After becoming a mother, I had to closely evaluate the storage use at home. I had no garage and once I had three children, there really was no space. I had to significantly cull my resources. Luckily, this was also at a time that flexible learning was becoming more widely accepted and resources were easy to store online. I donated lots of my teaching resources and got rid of things I didn't need. It was quite a revitalising experience to have less clutter in both my home and classroom. It made me focus on using high-quality resources and being more sustainable in my practices.

If you are keen on trying a minimalist approach to teaching, I highly recommend learning more about it. Removing teaching resources from the home is also a beneficial way to keep work and home separate, which is good for maintaining a positive work-life balance.

Storeroom example 1

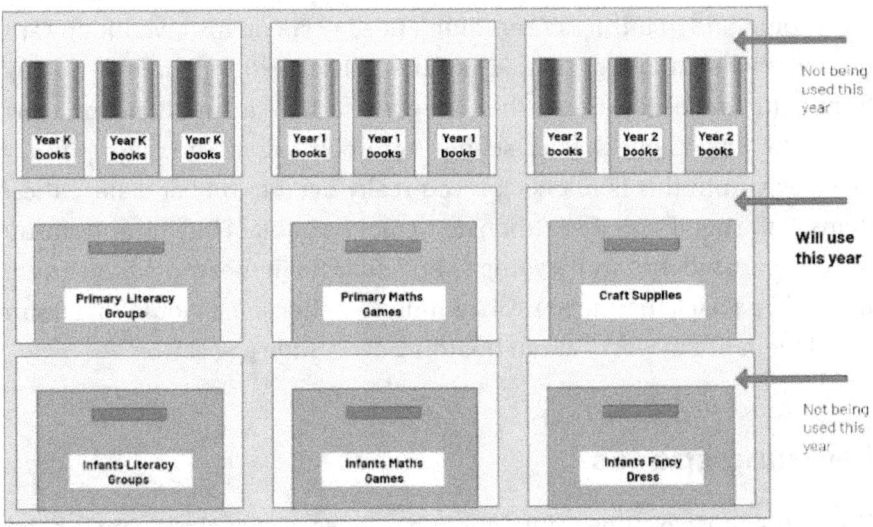

Storeroom example 2

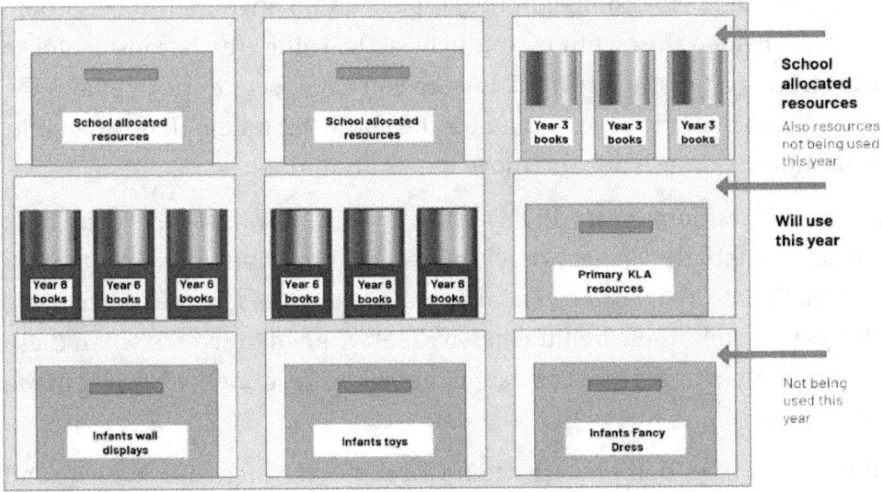

Taking on this approach meant I focused on keeping resources that were better quality and highly functional. I adopted a process of using school resources more. Schools often spend a large budget on resources that go unused when not utilised if teachers are buying many of their own resources. Many items I had in my storeroom could be easily accessed in school supplies. Things like paint, cardboard, pipe cleaners, pop sticks, etc, I could find in the art store. I didn't need to spend my own money and purchase when they were already available. If these things aren't available from your school resources, then it's good to have a supply in your own store. But always check your school storerooms first. The main point to take away from this is to check if you really need to buy and store these items. If the need isn't there, then don't make a habit of buying and storing things your students aren't going to benefit from in the immediate future. If I could go back in time to my beginning teacher self, I would make sure to tell them not to worry about hoarding every little egg carton.

Learning spaces

One of the most exciting things about having your own classroom is being able to make it your own learning space. Classrooms around the world vary and, in my experience, I've taught in large, brand-new classrooms and old, very small classrooms. Both designs can be a wonderful classroom space, provided the layout is conducive to learning. The hardest factor to deal with is often the furniture. Ensure you get a feel for the light and the sound, and take the time to plan for the space. Sit on the floor, at a table, walk around, draw it out and move things around.

In some classrooms you will have very uniform furniture where the desk heights match, the chairs are all the same colour and all your tote trays match. For me, that has been a rarity and as educators, we often like those things to match. There's a little itch we feel we need to scratch when these things don't match. I can't explain it, but it's there, nonetheless. Try not to scratch it.

If your tote trays don't match, then you can make matching labels – and make them big enough to cover most of the tray. If your table heights don't match, then this might be a sign to use some innovative designing on where you place those tables (or if you even use them at all). If your chairs don't match, you could create a quirky space where chairs are mixed up or possibly make some chair covers that include storage for student pencil cases.

These are just a few suggestions. I urge you to look at these inconsistencies as opportunities to be creative, rather than a hindrance to creating a great learning space. Many teachers in the early years get caught in the thought process "But my tables don't match, how am I meant to make table groups?". This kind of thought process will be interrupted the first time you have an exceptionally tall – or short – student who couldn't fit in that furniture anyway.

Stock standard furniture is slowly becoming a thing of the past as the world moves towards the use of flexible learning, and with it, flexible furniture. If your school has not yet begun this process, it doesn't matter – you can still create a flexible learning space regardless of the furniture you have. It's how you use it that matters.

Here are just a few examples of how you could arrange classroom furniture. What you use should best suit your students.

Traditional classroom layout

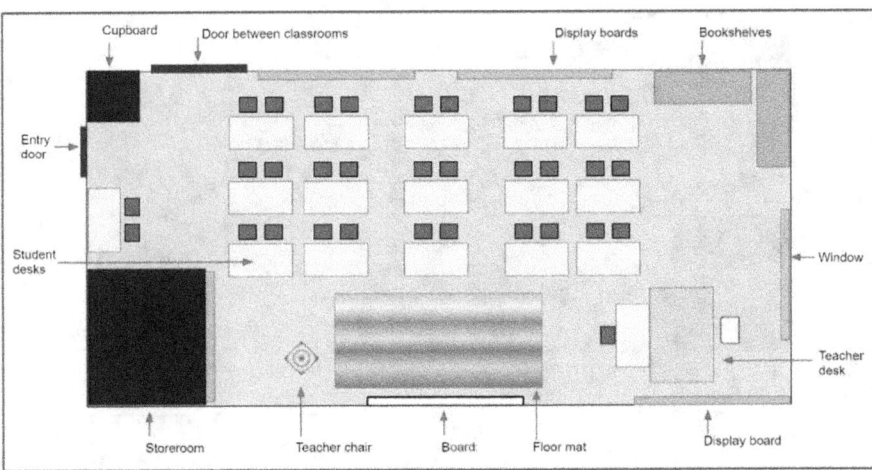

I call this style 'Traditional' in terms of its basic and functional layout. This essentially fits as many kids as possible into a room facing the teacher and the chalkboard. Notice I said 'chalkboard' – it's a bit old school. This style was often used as it was seen to minimise disruptions or talking during lessons. The teacher desk at the front so the teacher can monitor the class while they work. Very conducive for 'Chalk and Talk' style teaching.

A chair at the front with some carpet space, or a mat, for when the teacher would read a story to the class or have some whole-class discussion time. A teacher desk at the front and to the side so the teacher could get work done and be able to conference with students, while still being able to supervise the class. This layout can be difficult for students to see the materials presented at the front, or displayed around the room, depending on their seat.

This is not my preferred classroom layout, as it does not allow for much flexibility or quality collaboration, and it keeps the teacher very removed from the student workspace. Students at the back could feel detached from the teaching and learning, and it limits their opportunity to interact in classroom discussions or activities taking place at the front. It is very much a teacher-centred space.

U shape classroom layout

If you have fewer tables or students, the U shape can also be used without the additional tables in the centre section, as shown in the image. This design still allows for the teacher chair out the front and a mat for students to sit on. It still has a teacher desk and makes sure students are mostly facing the front. This design means you can spread students across the space of the room, and possibly limit any clashes in students who do not work well together – especially when students sitting in the middle section will have their backs to a student behind them.

A benefit to this design is that students can be close to any wall displays you have around the room and only need to turn to access any resources you have available, such as anchor charts or prompts. If your displays are large, then students will still be able to see displays on the other walls around the classroom. The teacher can move around the U shape to support students.

The disadvantage to this design is that it limits movement around the classroom, which can minimise how well you coordinate group tasks. You can move chairs around to allow this to happen, it just means making sure the class is well-trained in how to move the furniture quickly and responsibly. It would also mean prepping the class for additional movement or distractions, for example, students using the bookshelves while others are still working at their table nearby.

Table groups classroom layout

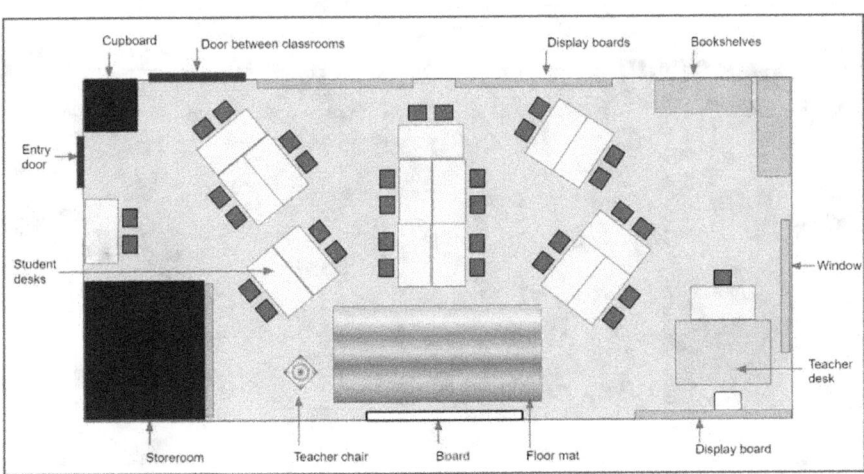

The table groups layout is a flexible option and allows more movement within the classroom. If you have allocated spaces for students, you can still reconfigure student groupings for certain tasks, and they have the functionality within the classroom to do that without the added task of moving chairs and tables. For example, students might stay in their allocated seating for most Key Learning Areas, but will change groups and work with different students for literacy or maths groupings.

In this configuration the tables are still directed to the front board as a focal point. Some students are seated more side-on, and some are facing the front directly. In this layout it is highly recommended that any students with glasses or sight needs are seated facing front-on to reduce any additional issues with their access in seeing the teacher or the material being presented.

When using the groups layout, it provides flexibility for how many students you have in groups. Some students work well in large numbers and others prefer small group numbers. You don't have to make them all the same and so there are some options there to monitor student interactions and how they best work in group scenarios. The difficulty may be the size of the room and you might need to play with moving the tables around to make it work well.

Flexible learning spaces layout

This is one of my favourite ways to create a comfortable learning space – but that does not mean it is the best. A flexible learning space takes time for students to adjust to if they are not used to it. It means building lots of trust and high expectations with your class. It involves student input into the learning space and providing choices for where and how they would like to learn. A flexible learning space has options for independent, pair, group and whole-class learning. There is no front or back. Just learning spaces.

A flexible learning space provides options for sitting, standing or alternative options. This does not need furniture specific to flexible learning, although it makes the process a bit easier – such as tables and chairs with adjustable height options. It can be created using a mixture of furniture such as a table from an older grade to use as a standing desk, or a table from a younger grade to use with cushions as a low table option. My rule with my students was: "As long as you are doing your best learning, then you get to choose where you learn; if you're not doing your best learning, then I get to choose a place for you."

The design in the diagram above was used in a Year 2 class and did not use any new furniture, but utilised mixed furniture from around the school. When creating a flexible learning space, always check any mandatory furniture regulations with your school system.

Perspective from the intervention table

Perspective from the entry door

These are photos of the flexible learning space used with a Year 2 class and mapped in the diagram on page 14. Every day, furniture could be moved around the room to allow students to engage in their learning. The cushions could be moved to the floor for sitting on. The mats on the floor could be dragged to a new space if a group wanted to play a maths game together. The standing table was on wheels and could be rolled around to fit more people around it – and it also had storage trays in it with resources for easy access.

This space changed each term based on feedback from the students. The curved table was used for intensive teaching and was placed near the storeroom at the beginning of the year. I had a reflection session with the class about the learning space and asked for their feedback about the space and any changes they recommended. They drew bird's-eye view maps of the classroom with their preferences. Almost the whole class identified that they didn't like where the intensive table was as they couldn't access their reading support materials during guided reading or writing sessions – which were on the other side of the room. We moved the table to where it is in these pictures. Student voice is vital to flexible learning.

Learning walls

Being able to decorate and rearrange the space is as exciting as moving out of home for the first time. I had spent four years at university saving all sorts of posters, pillows and wall décor for when this time arrived and when it happened, I may have gone a little overboard. Lots of motivational quotes, times table charts, planet posters, world maps all over the walls and windows.

I learned in the many years to come that less is more, and the greatest feature in any classroom is what the students create. It's very important that you embrace the ownership over this space and take the opportunity to make it your own. I recommend having a 'base coat' when you first start with your own classroom. Some basic materials that will make the room feel inviting but leaves space for development between you and the students. If you prepare titles, labels or borders for the work that is to come across the term, that is a good starting point to establish the expectation that the students will be contributing to that learning space – because the walls are indeed a learning space, not just for displays.

Be mindful of cognitive load of students and what information is necessary for them to be constantly exposed to throughout the day. Does a Year 6 class really need the alphabet poster on the wall? Are the students accessing that poster of the solar system for their learning this term? Do you need 30 motivational quotes on that one wall all year long? Really focus on that display material and ask yourself:

- What is this for and how is it being used?
- Is it relevant to our current learning?
- How do I know the students are using this?
- Did the students contribute to this resource?

Once you've answered these, then it will help in identifying what is pertinent to keep up, and how long to keep it up for. Those 30 motivational quotes might be more impactful if there was one display spot and quotes are rotated each week.

Additional spaces (extra room)

You may be fortunate to have a classroom that has an additional learning space attached to it. This could be a small room adjoining the classroom through an inner door. Many refer to this as a withdrawal space or quiet room. When I went to primary school it was called a Wendy House because it was where all the toys were kept for playing with – much like a cubby house; in my youth cubby houses were called Wendy Houses in reference to the little house that was built for Wendy in the children's story *Peter Pan*.

Even today, some teachers use this space as a room for playing. Some are used as a quiet space for taking a break. Many use it as a computer space. It is important to make sure you check if there are expectations in your school for the use of this space. Sometimes it is established as a computer space because that's where the technology cable points are located. A school may have a specific approach to behaviour where a quiet space is specifically designed for student emotional regulation needs. If you have a space like this, ensure you set expectations with the class for its use. Sometimes it can be hard to monitor this space as it is out of sight, and you won't move around in there as much as the rest of the classroom. Check in on it regularly to keep it tidy and functional.

Teacher desk

Ugh! Burn it! OK, I'm kidding... slightly. One of the best things I ever did was ditching the big, clunky teacher desk. It was nothing but a black hole of papers and stationery. I got rid of it and my classroom felt 10 times bigger! I put most things into the storeroom and kept one teacher tote tray that had my stickers, pens, awards, etc. If you have a desk or feel the need for one, I recommend keeping it minimal and functional. I recognise adults need adult furniture to work at when programming, etc, so if your desk is to suit your needs, then evaluate its size and placement in the class.

Students can find the teacher desk quite intimidating depending on the experiences they've had with that space. It can be a very positive space, too, if you design it to be so. Keeping positive reinforcement in that space, such as school awards and stickers, will help students maintain a positive mindset about the area. Ensuring that feedback provided in that space is linked directly to the lesson and focuses on learning goals will also help students develop a productive relationship with you in that space. It is important to ensure the desk doesn't become a barrier between you and the students.

Tip 1 summary

- Keep your storage tidy and clearly labelled to separate personal resources and school-allocated resources.

- It's best to avoid hoarding resources where possible. Utilise your school resources as much as you can.

- Take the time to plan your classroom set-up by mapping it out and consider all areas in the room as a possible learning space. Do this regularly over the year.

- Consider the layout of furniture and try some different designs to see what best suits your current class.

- Don't overload the classroom walls with massive amounts of resources – keep analysing the purpose of any displays you have and consider their value and the contribution made to them by the students.

- Include the students in the creation of learning displays.

- Plan out your additional learning spaces with intention and regularly check them for maintenance or upkeep.

- Having a teacher desk depends on your own style. I recommend trying with it, and without it, to see the difference it can make in your learning space.

- A classroom is a home away from home, and for many kids you will be providing a more comfortable space than their actual home. Always remember that.

Tip 2

Know your way around

When you first begin in a school, one of the things that is easy to skim over is taking some genuine time to get your bearings. My mentor once told me that it takes at least 18 months to get settled into a new school (even if you're the Principal) and I absolutely agree. There are lots of great resources that get collected and stored in schools, and many useful goodies hiding away in storerooms just waiting for a teacher to come and use them.

Even in a small school there are so many places that can often go unknown if someone doesn't show you that they exist. I had been working in a school for eight years and never knew we had an 'artefact storeroom' until I was put in charge of creating a history book for the school's 75th anniversary. I had walked past this door for eight years with no idea what was behind it! I honestly thought it was a cleaner's storeroom. When I eventually went in, it was full of amazing history, and I learned a great deal from those artefacts.

As a new teacher, it's important to seek out the physical environment, explore your school, and learn where everything is. This way you won't miss out on everything it has on offer. If this information isn't provided to you, then don't be afraid to ask. Some schools have an induction program; if your school doesn't, then talk to your supervisor, your teacher neighbour, an experienced member of staff, the General Assistant or even the lovely admin staff. Get a map of the school and note down everything that you think would be beneficial for you or your class. It might be beneficial to book in a specific time with one of these staff members to take some genuine time to have a proper tour and even hear some interesting history about your school. You never know how relevant that information can be as you become immersed in your school.

Staffroom

There are many spaces in your school that serve both the needs of the students and teachers. Be mindful that these spaces are the workstations for other staff and should be cared for the same way you wish your classroom to be cared for. If you need to use something in the administration space, check what the process is for doing so. For example, schools will have a process for the use of the school photocopier or laminator. This could mean leaving the task for an allocated admin staff and waiting for it to be completed, or you might be allowed to use the facilities yourself. There are often instructions for how to use these facilities. Make sure you read them first and notify an admin person if there are any issues. It is poor form to leave a photocopier without any paper in the tray or to leave a paper jam for someone else to remove – it's usually easy to figure out who did it when the paper jam is removed and '2W Homework' is on the sheet being printed. The same goes for leaving the laminator turned on after you've finished – that's a fire hazard.

Get to know where all the other classes are and see if you can get a class list with teachers' first and last names. Hopefully, you will receive a school map with this information during your induction. I find I always learn my colleagues' first names quickly and then when it's time to ask a student to take something to another class I have a mind blank on their last name and it goes something like: "Can you take this book back to Miss aaahhh, uuummm. You know, the kindy teacher, with the dark, curly hair."

FOR FORK'S SAKE, BRING YOUR OWN FORK! School kitchens are a black hole for utensils... and chocolate. You can never rely on a school cutlery drawer for a fork. I recommend buying one of those camp sets and keeping it safe somewhere for lunchtime. Put your name on your food in the fridge – especially if you're leaving butter or milk in there. Be a courteous colleague and cover dishes in the microwave and never leave something unwashed in the sink. Wash as you go – even if there is a diswasher. Always check the fridge regularly to see if you have forgotten your leftovers. Or, if by some miracle you find a fork and use it... RETURN IT!

Playground

The playground can be an interesting space to navigate depending on the layout of your school. Your first playground duty will feel a little crazy, especially when Kindergarten first joins you in the playground at break time. Take the time in those first days to walk around and get your bearings. See if there are any lines marked as 'out of bounds' and identify little pocket areas that might be an issue for your line of sight when on duty, such as bushes where kids might run behind during playtime. You should be provided with a school map that includes allocated play spaces – if you don't, please suggest this to your supervisor to help new staff. You will ease any nerves on those first days if you at least remember where you are.

The playground space will naturally evolve and develop its own little zones for types of play. Generally, you can split these between active and passive play areas. These areas can develop because of the natural environmental elements or because of the design and layout of the area. Take some time to notice how kids are playing in certain areas and this will help you know where to target your supervision throughout your playground duties.

Passive play can be found in places like a sandpit, picnic tables, covered spaces or if ground markings encourage quiet play with partners or small groups, such as hopscotch. Active play will most likely be found in areas designed to support large-group games or team play, such as play equipment, a basketball court or soccer field. In these spaces, kids will run around at full speed, without looking where they are going, and sports equipment will likely be thrown around just as fast as the kids. Don't supervise within close proximity to these kids. Closely watch them, but step back aways – the experience of a basketball to the face while wearing wire-rimmed sunglasses is NOT an experience you will enjoy. Trust me.

The playground is essentially an outdoor classroom. It is where kids learn how to socialise and engage in unstructured play. Utilise the space as best as you can whether it is for a lunch break or during a class lesson. It is a whole-school resource, so check if there is a booking system for using allocated areas during class time.

Spaces for learning

Outdoor spaces are a great asset for learning with many benefits. They get kids into natural lighting, fresh air and provide lots of opportunities to apply learning to real-world scenarios. They are most heavily connected with physical education activities, but also enable you to deeply connect with all Key Learning Areas. You can have science lessons while connecting with the natural world, mathematics conversations about patterns in built and natural environments, enjoy art lessons using mixed mediums – and let's not forget the experience of reading a book under the shade of a gum tree.

I highly encourage you to utilise as many outdoor spaces as you can once you are comfortable to do so. This will require setting expectations with your class before retreating to some outdoor learning. Even with older students who might be used to using outdoor spaces for learning, it is important to take the time to set up expectations when moving beyond the classroom space for learning. It is important to set expectations with the class before moving them outdoors. Be very clear about moving between the classroom and the space you will be working in. State the purpose of the lesson and why it will be held outside the classroom space. Reiterate to the class that even though the space has changed that they are still at school and the school expectations still apply. Ask students for feedback about where they like to learn outside to gauge productive spaces.

There are still some small schools that don't have a school hall. You will find them holding outdoor concerts and assemblies, which may be cancelled due to wet weather. But if your school has one, they are a great asset to support learning and activities for the school. They are great for performances, guest speakers, after-school activities, parent forums and professional learning meetings. As a class teacher, you might need to book this space for use during the day if you want to run a class lesson or perhaps hold a choir rehearsal on a regular basis. As mentioned earlier, check organisational processes with your supervisor or admin team prior to planning use of the hall.

When taking your class to the hall for a lesson, use the same outdoor lesson advice to set class expectations prior to changing location with the class. The hall is a large space that echoes, and every kid has some kind of primal urge to run and slide on a slippery hallway floor. Especially if they are taking off shoes for a gymnastics session. It's super fun to watch them fly across the space with their hair in the wind and a massively goofy grin on their face – but it's not worth the incident report you'll be filling in later when they've broken an arm or smacked heads with another kid and chipped a tooth. Set clear expectations that the hall is another learning space and make it clear why and how you are using the hall for learning.

The school hall is a great place to retreat to if you have a lesson that requires a lot of space. For example, a maths lesson on distance and you're making paper planes to fly. The kids will be noisy with excitement making the planes and they will want to test their plane over and over before taking some official measurements for the task. Take their mathematics books with them, take some measurement tools (tapes, metre rulers, etc). It's perfectly fine for them to sit on their floor to record their results. This reduces the impact of the noise your class may produce for your neighbour classes, and you will get higher engagement knowing the kids have more opportunity to really fly those planes far. If you plan ahead, you can mark out some 1m increments on the floor with some tape and save the time it will take to measure each one. As always, check first if this is OK to do on the floor. Some don't like the residue tape can leave behind if the floor has a certain polish. A way around this is simply using easy-to-remove tape such as painter's or electrical tape.

The library is another amazing learning space within a school. Many would call it the hub of the school. Everyone has a reason to love the library. There are books, computers, games, reading nooks and game centres. My previous school library had a piano! Libraries have come a long way since I began teaching and have a very strong focus on future-focused and innovative learning experiences. No longer is the library a place where you are shooshed! It is a place of versatile learning and collaboration.

Storerooms

Most schools will have allocated spaces for storing school resources – especially resources that are valuable or highly sought after. These can include physical materials for student use or resources you can use for modelling lessons. For example, in a mathematics storeroom you will likely find counters, number charts, 3D shapes and random containers that have been saved for measurement activities. It is beneficial to check where storerooms are located and what resources a school has before spending money to stock up on your own. Some schools might focus on resources in certain learning areas, such as literacy and numeracy, and other schools may have the budget to have a storeroom for all areas of learning, such as performance costumes.

Schools will have their own system for borrowing and utilising resources, such as a loan system through their library or a record sheet with details of who has borrowed what and when. Become familiar with these systems before borrowing and chat with your teaching team to ensure planning for teaching doesn't conflict with the need to share resources across the classes. There are some schools that don't use an official borrowing record and it runs on an honesty system. Be mindful not to abuse this system and return resources as soon as you are finished with them.

If something happens to get damaged either by yourself or a student, notify your supervisor straight away to ensure a replacement can be sourced quickly. Your executive team understands accidents happen and sometimes funds are held in case of damage. It's best to be honest about it immediately to ensure students aren't left without learning materials.

Many schools have a storeroom in the office for supplies and materials needed daily such as pens, pencils, rulers, etc. Ask your colleagues or supervisor at the start of the year if there is a class allocation of resources and if replenishment is available throughout the year. This will help you map out any planning for new materials across the year and if you would prefer to top up any resources with materials of your own choosing.

Movement around the school

Your class will need to move around the school before, during and after the school bell. There might be whole-school expectations in place for movement around the school and perhaps signage in the school, such as 'walk in the halls' or 'walk left on stairs'. This is something that you should explicitly model with your class when it moves from one space to another within the school. By modelling this with your whole class, students will know the expectation if they are walking with a partner or small group.

Sometimes it can be hard to keep a class monitored during this movement, and kids know it! If there are some kids keen for a chat during these times, they will utilise those few minutes if you are walking at the front of the line with your back to the class. I recommend assigning some 'line leaders' as part of class responsibilities (which can rotate as you wish – I like weekly). These leaders are responsible for modelling sensible movement from one space to another, following the school expectations. Kids love responsibility like this. Then you can walk at the back of the line, keeping a safe eye on the whole class as they walk, and monitor appropriate movement.

If the school doesn't have designated 'stop points', I recommend designing some – with the students if they are old enough to know the school spaces well. Stop points are the places that the class will pause to wait for the remainder of the class or for the teacher to move to the front to give instructions. For example, you ask your class to line up behind the line leaders at the classroom door. From there, you ask the line leaders to walk down the corridor and stop at the turn in the corridor (this would be the 'stop point'). You can walk behind the class to monitor, then, as the line stops behind the leaders, you can walk to the front of the line and provide the class with any instructions if needed. Then the leaders walk to the next stop point, which might be near a designated class, bush, path, etc. You can stand still and watch the class pass you, as they follow the leaders, and join the end of the line to continue monitoring as needed.

Display boards

There are a few different types of display boards in a school. There are those used in the classrooms and learning spaces, boards in the hallways, the office will have some and your staffroom might have some, too. How these are used will often differ across schools, so please don't feel silly for asking what the expectation or process is for the use of these boards.

In your classroom, it's usually your own decision to use these, but it doesn't hurt to check. For the boards beyond the classroom, there is sometimes an expectation to display some work from your class. This might rotate through classes, or you might be asked to update an allocated space once a term with a new display. It is important not to create extra work for yourself or the students for this space. Share something genuine from your class that they are learning about. The kids love sharing off their work. If you have a creative flair and enjoy designing the display, I highly recommend including photos of the kids completing the work that is on display.

If there is a message board for parents and community, this is a great place to put reminders about excursions or special events. If you are part of an organising committee or if your class is involved in anything special, then this spot is a good place to advertise for parents who regularly visit the school. Otherwise, a digital display board is also beneficial for those parents engaging in an online communication platform, such as ClassDojo or Seesaw.

The office administration area is often a place for messages for teachers and sometimes displaying student work. As a new member of staff, please ensure you know what messages are displayed where. Some are for daily communication that you will likely check each morning for updates, such as duty changes or absences that might impact your timetable. Other display boards will include information about work, health and safety, Union information, social club updates or perhaps staff shout-outs. If you are looking for certain information and can't find it, let your supervisor or an executive know, as they may not be aware that it is missing for new staff members.

Local community

Beyond the school you will be surrounded by your local community. This could be very close to the school if you are in a metropolitan area, or it could be sparse if your school is regional or remote. Either way, regardless of distance, that is your local school community. It's important that you get to know what and who is in this space and how you can work together to support both school and community.

This can include shops, businesses, local council, library, waterways, sports grounds, parks and many more. Your local emergency services could be located nearby or even your local MP. There is much to be gained by developing good relationships with those close to the school setting for both the school and the local network. If there is a local catering business, it will appreciate your support for staff lunches or special events. The local emergency services may be able to support you during your evacuation drills. The local butcher or baker might be willing to donate some food for the next school BBQ fundraiser.

Knowing the area will support you in developing quality teaching and learning programmes that incorporate local knowledge and opportunities to easily accessible learning experiences. If you can build connections with local Aboriginal elders, their knowledge and expertise will greatly support you to enhance learning and forge positive relationships. Sometimes it's helpful to just walk the area that your students live in to develop a good understanding of their background and build relational trust with the community. Your students' parents and family might work locally or even own one of the local businesses, and showing them your support helps gain trust and develop ongoing relationships that support the school and your students.

It's beneficial to be aware of what communication goes to your local community for special events or updates in the area. This will help you promote them to the school, allowing your students the chance to access opportunities beyond the classroom, such as local festivals, competitions, sports, etc.

Tip 2 summary

- Know your way around by taking the time to roam and ask questions of your colleagues. Use the maps and visit other classes, even just to say hi! Don't skip alternate learning areas like the library, languages classroom or the canteen. They are all important to know.

- Use the staffroom with manners and remember it is a communal space for break time and work time. Don't assume something will get cleaned up for you in this shared space.

- The playground is like a classroom without borders. It can get hectic when not planned for. Yet it's still a space that should be used with guidelines and expectations.

- Spaces for learning can be indoors and outdoors, and all areas between the school gate and the classroom. Sometimes a change in scenery is a great break for the students and yourself, and can create a highly engaging experience for all involved. Plan for it, be mindful of other classes working nearby and be ready to change the plan if it's not working.

- Storerooms are not a free-for-all environment that has magic cleaning fairies. Use the materials within them the same way you would want other people to treat things they borrow from you. Follow school processes for using materials within storerooms and be honest about damage.

- Classes need to move around the school, and you are responsible for showing them explicitly how to do so in a safe and respectful manner. Be vigilant... and quiet.

- Displays are a great way to communicate and showcase work – but don't let it overload your teaching priorities.

- The local community is your student's life and support. Build relationships with the community and you will create great opportunities for your school.

Tip 3

Start your program with skeletons

Programming will likely be the largest portion of your administrative load. But there are very good reasons to program effectively, and if you dedicate the appropriate time to it, you will refine your skills and your students will benefit from your preparation. It's a great opportunity to combine the curriculum with your unique perspective and interpretation of quality learning and teaching. It does get quicker over time once you have found a method that suits your teaching style, and you develop a routine.

A teaching program is a legal document, so when you are compiling your program you need to always be aware that it is the property of your employer and always subject to review. While it is valuable to have your own interpretation and personal input into a program, there are mandatory requirements for educational programs. Each state or education system will have differences in the mandatory requirements of programs and it's very important that teachers remain up to date on policy changes within their own system and state.

In my day, I used to spend hours indulging in printing out pictures I liked to glue on a folder, cover in contact and then make very creative title pages for each section of my program. Now I program digitally using OneNote and I LOVE it – I do miss all my cool printed folder covers, though.

Ideally, a program should be able to be picked up by a colleague and taught without much explanation. It should clearly demonstrate what the students have learnt, their current level of achievement based on assessments, what they need to learn next and how that learning will occur in line with curriculum expectations and the differentiation needed for any complexities within your class.

Class profile overview

A class profile is comprised of short and sharp information that captures your class in a succinct manner. It does not cover detailed information about each student, but provides some key information as a summary of your class and your students' needs. You will see below a template of a class profile and, following that, an example of a completed class profile. Your school context might require the need for additional columns of information, or you can otherwise use the notes column on the far right to include some specific details. The class profile overview is a handy way to start to develop an understanding of your class before going deeper with knowledge of them as individuals. This sheet can also be helpful for any relief teachers working in the class who may not know your students. Do not put sensitive or confidential information in this overview if it is going to be seen by staff who should not be privy to that information. Instead, you can leave a comment in the notes section such as *'Please see the class supervisor for more information.'*

The completed class overview uses colour coding for house colours and bright red to note students who do not have permission to publish. This is important in case there is a school event, and a relief teacher is taking the class during a time when photography could occur. The codes in use are purely based on personal preference – unless you are in a school where codes are part of the school expectation for documentation or communication. There are often occasions when you will need to know each student's specific age, such as sporting events, so having that entered at the beginning of the year will save you some time for those occasions. Some other categories you might like to include are left-/right-handed, siblings in school, or if your school has a high number of new arrival students, you might like to include their date of arrival in the country.

Class Profile Overview template

Year:			Grade:			Class:				Teacher:	

#	Name	Birthday	Age this year	House	Permission to publish	Medical	EALD	PLP	IEP	Glasses	Notes
1											
2											
3											
4											
5											
6											
7											
8											
9											
10											
11											
12											
13											
14											
15											
16											
17											
18											
19											
20											
21											
22											
23											
24											
25											
26											
27											
28											
29											
30											
31											

Key	House groups:	Medical:	EALD:	IEP:

Class Profile Overview – example

Year: 2023 **Grade:** 2 **Class:** 2W **Teacher:** Mrs West

#	Name	Birthday	Age this year	House	Permission to publish	Medical	EALD	PLP	IEP	Glasses	Notes
1	Liam	14/6/2016	7	R	Y		Vietnamese	Y			
2	Oliver	20/9/2015	8	R	Y	Asthma			Y ASD	Y	
3	Noel	1/6/2016	7	B	Y						
4	Elijah	6/2/2016	7	B	Y		Mandarin TN				Out of Home Care (OOHC)
5	Susan	3/8/2015	8	Y	Y						
6	Kate	2/11/2015	8	R	Y			Y			
7	Heidi	6/7/2015	8	Y	N	Asthma		Y		Y	
8	Lauren	13/2/2016	7	Y	Y						
9	John	25/9/2015	8	R	Y		Vietnamese				New arrival
10	Adam	22/3/2016	7	G	Y				Y Sp		
11	Logan	1/6/2016	7	G	Y	Diabetes 2					
12	Xavier	7/3/2016	7	G	Y						Attends OOSH after school
13	Kathleen	5/2/2016	7	B	Y						
14	Betty	16/7/2015	8	B	Y						
15	Lillian	28/9/2015	8	R	Y	ANA: eggs	Arabic TN				
16	Esther	30/12/2015	8	G	Y				Y ADHD	Y	
17	Alison	31/4/2016	7	Y	N						
18	Lyndall	12/2/2016	7	R	Y		Vietnamese				
19	Ly	1/6/2016	7	G	Y						
20	Stephen	4/3/2016	7	G	Y	ANA: nuts					
21	Dean	8/8/2015	8	B	Y						
22	Nathan	4/10/2015	8	B	Y		Samoan TN				
23	Andrew	14/3/2016	7	Y	Y						
24	Jeffrey	21/10/2015	8	B	N				Y ASD	Y	Court order – Dad no contact
25	Jaye	20/2/2015	8	Y	Y						
26	Kim	2/12/2015	8	Y	Y	AL: carpet	Vietnamese				
27	Tara	7/1/2016	7	G	Y				Y Sp		
28	Cindy	29/7/2015	8	G	Y						
29	Alicia	1/3/2016	7	R	Y		Cantonese				
30	Courtney	6/11/2015	8	B	Y		Arabic	Y			
31	Jackie	3/4/2016	7	G	Y				Y Sp		

Key
House groups: R = Royal, B = Bogus, G = Gang, Y = Yolo
Medical: ANA = anaphylaxis, ALL = allergy
EALD: TN = translator needed for parent communication
IEP: ASD = autism spectrum disorder, Sp = speech diagnosis, ADHD = attention deficit hyperactivity disorder

34 Talkin' Chalk

I recommend revisiting this profile each term, ensuring you include any new students to your class and save as a new file. I don't recommend deleting old versions, as that documentation is still important to keep as a record. Acronyms will vary between schools or systems.

Individualised plans

There are different types of individualised plans that are necessary for supporting student needs. These may include:

Individual Education Plan (IEP)

An IEP is designed for students with a formal diagnosis or students identified with additional needs that may not yet have a diagnosis. It identifies goals using input from the teacher, parents and any specialists involved. The school counsellor or psychologist would assist in the development of this plan along with relevant members of the school learning support team. Goals can focus on academic needs or include other areas of development relevant to the student, such as fine or gross motor skills. It must include a review schedule and be updated throughout the year. If goals are attained, then they are reviewed, revised and updated accordingly.

Individual Behaviour Plan (IBP)

An IBP is very similar to an IEP, except that the goals are primarily focused on behavioural development. This also can be designed with the same key stakeholders to the students as would be in the IEP, as well as also following a review schedule regularly throughout the year. An IBP may also be accompanied by a risk assessment if the student behaviour is deemed unsafe. It may also include a chart where trigger behaviours are listed and various strategies for de-escalating behaviours are provided.

Personalised Learning Pathway (PLP)

A PLP is designed to increase engagement for Aboriginal students. It is a tool to support students in enhancing their educational outcomes and developing connections with community. There is no set template for a

PLP and can be customised by schools to meet the needs of the students and the school context. They may include academic goals and cultural goals. A PLP is developed using a three-way process between student, teacher and parents.

This template can be edited and adjusted to an IBP or PLP by modifying cells as needed. If your school already has a template in place, ensure you are using school documentation as required.

The documentation of program adjustments or modifications for student learning is part of mandated documentation requirements and will support the school learning support team in meeting the requirements for the National Consistent Collection of Data (NCCD) process. This type of planning and documentation also supports your school learning support team in making applications for student support through funding programs and accessing relevant professional learning for staff in your school.

The time required to complete this type of documentation can be cumbersome at times, especially when you're not used to compiling documents like this. Please connect with the school learning support team to ask for assistance when starting out.

Over the following pages is a completed example of an IEP designed purely for this book – it is not based on a particular student. I did not need to redact any information. If you were sharing this in a school-based scenario, you must be mindful of any sensitive or confidential information that might be included in the plan.

There might be circumstances where you are working with your teaching team about class needs, and even though that is a safe space to discuss the needs in your class, you must always be mindful about what information is shared, when it is shared and why it is shared. Sometimes this can be tricky to navigate in complex cases and the support of your teaching team is vital, but a student's confidentiality is of utmost importance, and we must do what we can to adhere to that.

Individual Education Plan template

Name:	DOB:	Grade/class:	Teacher:	IEP start date:	IEP review dates:
Diagnosis/disability confirmation		Funding		School support	External support

Student strengths			Student interests		

Student goals		Parent goals		Teacher goals	

Additional information:

SMART GOALS – Specific, Measurable, Actionable, Relevant, Timely

Focus area	SMART goal	Strategies/adjustments	Responsibility	Monitoring

Review meetings

Date/time/staff	Review and evaluation of goals	Further action

Individual Education Plan – example

Name:	DOB:	Grade/class:	Teacher:	IEP start date:	IEP review dates:
Elijah Johns	6/3/2016	Year 1, 1/2W	Rebecca West	28/2/2022	Term 1, Week 10

Diagnosis/disability confirmation	Funding	School support	External support
Autism spectrum disorder	$8,043 (integration funding support)	LST, SLSO class support	NDIS – speech + occupational therapy

Student strengths	Student interests
Friendly and kind	Computers and computer games
Very positive attitude to school and learning	Trains (and various other transport)
Extremely creative with computer games and computers in general	Painting and drawing
Very good at reading	Spending time with family

Student goals	Parent goals	Teacher goals
To read harder books	Develop strong friendships	Comprehension skills – inferential specifically
To get better at handwriting	Build resilience when he fails/loses at something	Improve confidence in trying new things
Make more friends	Improve fine motor skills – writing/cutting	Improve fine motor skills
Get faster at running	Comprehension skills	Support development of friendships

Additional information:
Elijah has many friends at school and is well-liked by his peers. He seems to often spend his playtime with students in younger grades as he has found it difficult to manage challenging moments with children his own age. Elijah struggles to articulate his feelings when he is not managing a situation and finds this frustrating, so he enjoys playing with younger students as he does not encounter this issue as much with younger peers. Elijah gets along very well with peers in class time and enjoys participating in activities and discussions where teacher support enables a positive level of interaction with his peers. Sometimes Elijah finds the thought of failing or losing more challenging than when it actually happens, and this sometimes impacts his willingness to play with peers his own age.

SMART GOALS – Specific, Measurable, Actionable, Relevant, Timely

Focus area	SMART goal	Strategies/adjustments	Responsibility	Monitoring
Goal 1: Literacy – comprehension	By the end of Week 8, Term 2, Elijah will be able to read and comprehend a level 8 decodable text.	Elijah will participate in guided reading sessions four times per week with the class teacher. He will receive familiar reading sessions two times per week with an SLSO. He will receive allocated support time during literacy sessions to support comprehension tasks based on modelled and guided reading sessions over the term. Parents have agreed to read decodable texts with Elijah at home for at least 20 minutes per day and engage in asking questions and discuss the text.	Class teacher SLSO (parents)	Elijah will be monitored through ongoing observations by the class teacher and SLSO. Parents will submit reading logs weekly with homework. He will be assessed on reading fluency and comprehension using the Sparkle Kit.
Goal 2: Literacy – fine motor	By the end of Week 9, Term 1, Elijah will be able to independently trace over shapes and letters with at least 80% accuracy and write his own name independently.	Elijah will be provided with targeted fine motor tasks during literacy rotations and work 1:1 with the SLSO. Tasks will be based on fine motor skills that support hand development such as cutting, squishing, pinching, etc, as guided by his occupational therapist (example tasks in files). The SLSO will only use the hand-over-hand technique when providing explicit teaching strategies. Elijah will practise writing his name every day and be given tracing tasks within his homework in lieu of sentence writing. Parents have agreed to this substitute to prioritise fine motor development for this term.	Class teacher SLSO (parents)	Elijah will be monitored by collecting work samples regularly and monitoring the transference of skills to handwriting and writing sessions in class.
Goal 3: Social emotional – friendships	By the end of Week 9, Term 1, Elijah will learn key phrases to join games with peers near to his own age and apply these in both class and playground situations.	Elijah will participate in the social skills group program coordinated by the school psychologist. The program will run once a week for one hour with a small group of students near to Elijah's own age. Students will develop friendship skills related to the classroom and the playground. The class teacher and SLSO will receive resources and feedback from the school psychologist to ensure consistency of language and skill development throughout the program. The school psychologist and SLSO will also monitor for developments in the playground (timetable to be rescheduled).	School psychologist Class teacher SLSO	Elijah will be monitored through the social skills program, classroom/ playground observations and monitoring any records of incidents with other students. Elijah will have the opportunity to self-reflect during the social skills program. Parents will be asked of any change in situations outside school, for example, local park.
Goal 4: Social emotional – resilience	By the end of Week 8, Term 2, Elijah will be able to choose a learned technique when finding it difficult to remain calm during a situation related to loss or failure.	Elijah will participate in the class Welcome Circle and Smiling Minds, which the teacher will specifically design around resilience. The whole class will participate in sessions to learn about growth mindset and resilience. The teacher/SLSO will work in small groups where Elijah can participate with peers of his choosing that he feels safe with to engage in targeted activities that model breathing techniques, walk-away techniques and using key phrases to help calm down. The teacher will install an 'emotional thermometer' in the classroom and incorporate this resource into the school PBL lessons. The teacher will create anchor charts for the class and provide mini versions for Elijah's desk to support him in using techniques during challenging situations. The school psychologist will also use the same resources in their sessions during the social skills program.	Class teacher SLSO support School psychologist support	The teacher will monitor Elijah's development against previous records where checklists were used to record the regularity of incidents where Elijah did not participate due to fear of failure or had difficulty calming down. Teacher and SLSO will observe the use of techniques learned during class sessions and Elijah will be asked to self-reflect on how he feels when using the breathing or calming techniques.

Start your program with skeletons

SMART GOALS – Specific, Measurable, Actionable, Relevant, Timely continued...

Date/time/staff	Review meetings	
	Review and evaluation of goals	Further action
Term 1, Week 10 Tuesday Class teacher, SLSO, school psychologist, learning and support teacher, parents	**Goal 1: Literacy – comprehension.** Elijah can successfully read and comprehend a level 7 decodable text. **Goal 2: Literacy – fine motor.** Elijah can independently write his own name and trace over letters and shapes with 80% accuracy. **Goal 3: Social emotional – friendships.** Elijah has been able to use some of the strategies learned during the social skills group in the classroom setting and in the playground. He still needs some guidance and support from the teacher or from other peers who feel more confident using the strategies. **Goal 4: Social emotional – resilience.** Elijah has found it difficult to respond to the use of breathing techniques and says he finds it hard to focus on breathing when he is feeling overwhelmed. He has said he thinks everyone is looking at him when he is trying to calm down and would prefer to be alone and walk away. Elijah said he likes the emotional thermometer and the anchor charts on his desk.	**Goal 1:** Elijah will continue with guided reading groups, familiar reading and home reading next term. **Goal 2:** Elijah will continue this process with small words and drawings using shapes. **Goal 3:** Elijah will continue with the social skills program for five more weeks next term with some new students included in the program to support him transitioning these skills with new people. Parents report he has only tried these skills twice outside the school context, once was with family. **Goal 4:** Teacher will trial the use of a calm down space in the classroom of Elijah's choosing and print out the emotional thermometer and anchor charts to be placed in the calm down space. Teacher will create a flowchart with Elijah about the steps and expectations for using this space to calm down in difficult scenarios. School psychologist will also identify a place in the playground that is safe and appropriate for Elijah to calm down during playtime and print out the above resources to be placed in a playground location to support Elijah using these strategies.

Timetable/KLA distribution

When starting out the year, you will receive information about school timetables and schedules. This might only be a temporary schedule for the first couple of weeks or it could be for the term allocation. Be prepared for this to change. The first few weeks of the year are hectic, and families often move during the summer holidays and turn up to their local school to enrol on Day 1. Some turn up a few days after that. And then even more come a few weeks later. This can shift the class allocations around at the last minute. As much as this can be frustrating to experience, it really is out of anyone's hands and your leadership team will do what they can to keep you informed as changes occur.

I remember one year where I started with a Year 2/3 composite class; it was meant to be an extension class, and I was so excited to be doing something a bit different to what I had done before. Right at the end of Week 3, there was an influx of students and my class turned into a straight Year 3 class. This did make it much easier for programming, but I learned a hard lesson that year not to make, print and laminate multiple class sets of name tags, bookmarks and a class birthday chart right at the start of the year. I had to start all over again. This change for my class also meant a change across the whole school for timetable allocations for relief teachers, support allocations, language classes and scripture schedules. So, the timetable I was given in Week 1 was very different to the one I ended up with in Week 4. And, of course, that timetable changes over the year depending on the needs of the school – and how those needs fluctuate over the year with new enrolments, changes in staff, and of course the development of the students.

To start your base timetable, slot in sections you know have been allocated, such as, library, support, languages, scripture, release, sport, assembly, etc. Then you can work in your Key Learning Areas (KLAs) around those times. Sometimes the allocated support sessions will be helpful and other times it will feel challenging to fit sessions in a way that is conducive to your schedule. Using the mandated time allocations for your sector will help with this.

Weekly timetable template

	Mon	Tue	Wed	Thu	Fri
8:30–9am					
9–10am					
10–11am					
11–11:20am					
11:20–12:10pm	Lunch	Lunch	Lunch	Lunch	Lunch
12:10–1:10pm					
1:10–1:40pm					
1:40–2pm	Recess	Recess	Recess	Recess	Recess
2–3pm					
Meetings					
Notes					

Weekly timetable in progress – example

	Mon	Tue	Wed	Thu	Fri
8:30–9am		Admin meeting			
9–10am	Class roll Reading Spelling	Class roll Reading News groups	Class roll Library	Class roll Scripture Writing	Class roll Reading Spelling
10–11am	Fruit break Writing	Fruit break Writing	Fruit break Spelling	Fruit break Reading	Fruit break Health
11–11:20am	Handwriting	~~Buddy reading~~	Grammar	Fitness	Handwriting
11:20–12:10pm	Lunch	Lunch	Lunch	Lunch	Lunch
12:10–1:10pm	Maths	Maths	Maths	Maths	Sport
1:10–1:40pm	Science	Maths	Creative arts	Health	Sport
1:40–2pm	Recess	Recess	Recess	Recess	Recess
2–3pm	Science	Fitness	Creative arts	HSIE	Assembly
Meetings			STAFF PL – maths		
Notes	Ran out of time for handwriting	Buddy reading cancelled as teacher was sick			

Timetable in a daybook format – example

	Monday	To-do	Notes
8:30–9am		Laminate name tags	Ran out of time for handwriting
9–10am	Class roll Reading – Matilda, Chapter 4 Spelling – 'ai'	Submit PL application	
10–11am	Fruit break Writing – comic strips	Complete maths program for Week 7	
11–11:20am	Handwriting – clockwise letters	LST meeting follow-up with counsellor	
11:20–12:10pm	Lunch		
12:10–1:10pm	Maths – fractions		
1:10–1:40pm	Science – STEM lab with Mr T – Volcano!		
1:40–2pm	Recess		
2–3pm	Science – STEM lab with Mr T – Volcano!		
Meetings			

Scope and sequences, and units of work

Your school should have a scope and sequence of KLAs for your grade or stage allocation as part of the whole-school planning process. If this is not available to you, there are examples available online. In NSW, this is through the NSW Education Standards Authority (NESA). As I write this book, new curriculum is being created and implemented across NSW, so the examples provided may change with the new curriculum. But my point is that you should not take on the workload of developing a whole scope and sequence just for your class or your grade. That is a massive effort and requires a lot of detail, especially to meet mandatory programming requirements.

Once you have a scope and sequence available to you (whether it's a school one or a sample one), this is where you will be able to break down your year into chunks of time. Schools may have prepared units of work in line with their scope and sequence with the expectation that you use the prepared program and make modifications as needed for your class. Be prepared for the various opinions people have regarding programming.

At university you may have been exposed to a variety of lesson planning and programming styles. There is no one right way. What works for one teacher may not work for another. One teacher might develop an amazing program for their class, another retired teacher might be selling an amazing program for $10 on Teachers Pay Teachers. My biggest piece of advice I can give you is that your teaching will suffer if your workload suffers. There is no shame in utilising a great program that you find from somewhere else, providing you are not breaching any of your school requirements in the process.

You might really enjoy the process of developing a writing unit but experience challenges with writing maths programs. That's absolutely OK. You're a new teacher and still learning. If you need to use the downloaded unit to help you find your groove, then go for it. Use it and learn from it. The important part is to LEARN from it. Don't just download and teach without modifying or innovating it in your own way. Learn from it!

Assessment and data collection

Much like the scope and sequences, your school will also likely have an assessment schedule for the year. This will map out the assessments for the year, possibly narrowed down to a specific time frame, such as which week in which term it is expected to be assessed. When you are compiling your teaching programs, take the assessment schedule into account for your teaching time frame. You might have an awesome hands-on maths lesson on three-dimensional shapes planned for the same week a number assessment needs to be completed. This might mean refining your program timeline and also might mean reducing the number of lessons in that week to allow for the assessment to take place during that time.

Opposite, I've provided an assessment schedule that I compiled for sharing as an example with other school leaders. You can see how the weeks can build up with something almost every week. Some things are tasks that would be completed in a normal class session, such as a writing sample. Whatever is written in class that week becomes the sample. However, NAPLAN has a mandated date allocation and can only be completed in that time frame. That's an assessment that needs to be scheduled around.

Assessment schedule – example

Term	Wk	Kindergarten	Stage 1	Stage 2	Stage 3
1	1	Best Start Formal	AWESOME TEST		
	2		SENA	SENA	SENA
	3		SA Spelling	SA Spelling	SA Spelling
	4		Reading + comprehension	Reading + comprehension	Reading + comprehension
	5	Intervention Graphs	Intervention Graphs + PLAN 2	Intervention Graphs + PLAN 2	Intervention Graphs + PLAN 2
	6	Writing sample	Writing sample	Writing sample	Writing sample
	7	TEN	TEN	PAT-M	PAT-M
	8	Reading + PLAN 2	Reading + PLAN 2	Reading + PLAN 2	Reading + PLAN 2
	9	CTJ + Intervention Graphs/data	CTJ + Intervention Graphs/data	CTJ + Intervention Graphs/data	CTJ + Intervention Graphs/data
	10	Planning day	Planning day	Planning day	Planning day
2	1		Writing sample	Writing sample	Writing sample
	2		TEN	TEN/Maths diagnostic	Reading + comprehension
	3		Reading	Reading + comprehension	
	4			NAPLAN	NAPLAN
	5	Intervention Graphs + PLAN 2	Intervention Graphs + PLAN 2	Intervention Graphs + PLAN 2	Intervention Graphs + PLAN 2
	6			Maths diagnostic	Maths diagnostic
	7	Reports to supervisors	Reports to supervisors	Reports to supervisors	Reports to supervisors
	8	Reading + PLAN 2	Reading + PLAN 2	Reading + PLAN 2	Reading + PLAN 2
	9	CTJ + Intervention Graphs/data	CTJ + Intervention Graphs/data	CTJ + Intervention Graphs/data	CTJ + Intervention Graphs/data
	10	Planning day	Planning day	Planning day	Planning day

Notes

Intervention Graphs	Identify tier 1, 2 and 3 students (including extension) in the intervention chart with blue, green, yellow and red sections. Students listed as yellow on intervention graphs are prime subjects for PLAN 2 monitoring. Yellow students to have work samples and personalised learning goals on data wall – created and updated with it.
CTJ	Consistent Teacher Judgement – complete formative/summative assessment and analyse across the team. Update personalised learning goals during team planning with AP and IL.
PLAN 2	Review student data and update tracking on PLAN 2. Discuss changes to intervention graphs with AP/IL and update personalised learning goals on data wall.
TEN/PAT-M/diagnostic	Use the listed assessment tool for all students. Analyse data, collect work samples and create personalised numeracy goals with it.
Writing	Cold writing sample using a stimulus for whole class and assess against rubric. Shared marking between the grade/stage. Create personalised writing goals on data wall.
Reading/comp	PM reading level tracking (Kindy to include sounds and vocab assessments). Comprehensive rubric monitored once a term. Collect samples for data wall and creating of reading goals on data wall.
Reports	Academic reports due to supervisors – all grades and comments.

Start your program with skeletons

Accreditation (NSW)

Setting a goal like *'Achieve proficiency'* in your first year is a milestone that sets you up for a lot of unnecessary extra work at a time when you will already be in cognitive overload. Instead, I recommend *'Collect samples and annotations to complete more than half of my accreditation requirements.'* It's achievable because it keeps to this structure of just starting out with a skeleton and building on it as you can. I recommend using a digital diary to save your artefacts and annotations over time. See the template below:

STANDARD 1: Know students and how they learn

Focus area

1.1 Physical, social and intellectual development and characteristics of students
1.2 Understand how students learn
1.3 Students with diverse linguistic, cultural, religious and socioeconomic backgrounds
1.4 Strategies for teaching Aboriginal and Torres Strait Islander students
1.5 Differentiate teaching to meet the specific learning needs of students across the full range of abilities
1.6 Strategies to support full participation of students with disability

Focus area	Artefact 1	Artefact 2	Artefact 3	Artefact 4
1.1				
1.2				
1.3				
1.4				
1.5				
1.6				

There are templates for each of the seven standards provided in the templates section at the end of this book. To use the template, just copy your photo or screenshot into the appropriate cell and hit 'enter' to type an annotation below it. When you start doing this, I recommend just using dot points or key words to help get things going. When you have time to reflect properly and think of the language of the standards, then you will be able to write a more detailed annotation. You may decide over time that you have a better artefact to use, and you don't want to waste time typing a long annotation you might never use.

Professional Development Plan (PDP)

This may have different names in different school systems, but the gist of it is the same – set some professional goals for the year and identify things that will assist you in achieving those goals. When you start teaching, I recommend sticking to three goals only. Use the SMART goal method and keep it achievable. Setting a goal like *'Learn more maths strategies'* is very unclear and so broad it could lead you down a rabbit hole of professional learning. Think more specifically to be able to narrow it down. This will support the leadership team in providing professional learning that supports your goal progression and also helps reduce your cognitive load while learning something new. I would recommend instead a goal such as *'Refine strategies for introducing new measurement concepts.'*

Tip 3 summary

- Start your program with a skeleton structure. You do not need to have the entire year – or even the entire term – mapped out in detail. Give yourself room to breathe.

- Use templates and examples to help guide you along the way. As a new teacher you are learning, and it is perfectly fine to learn from the examples and support of the teachers who have been doing it for a while.

- Use the school-provided scope and sequences and teaching units where provided. Make modifications as you need, to support your students and document these changes as you go. If your school does not have these documents prepared, then utilise examples or prewritten units while you learn to develop your own.

- Check the assessment schedule against your units of work for the term to avoid clashes or overloading the teaching program.

- In your first year, accreditation will be on your mind. There is nothing to gain by rushing it. Save artefacts from time to time with some notes to fill out later.

- Keep goals simple and succinct; limit yourself to just three.

Tip 4

Plan for short-term and long-term organisation

Successful organisation is grounded in preparedness. In education this means being well aware of the expectations of your role as a teacher and the various elements of your responsibilities as an employee. Teaching is not a 9am to 3pm job. Teaching is a way of life, and it's a life that can leave you very time poor if you are underprepared. Being time poor leads to a poor balance between your personal and professional life, which can impact negatively on your mental and physical wellbeing.

As teachers, we spend many hours on organisation, but when it comes to being part of a school, there is more to it all than just what we do with our own class. Many whole-school events and activities can create an impact on your workload and sometimes these are things that happen repetitively, sometimes every year, such as carnivals, concerts, excursions, etc. You might be part of the committee, or you might just be a participant, but either way, you will need to have your class organised for the day.

Your level of organisation can impact or improve the way in which your students engage in these activities and events. If you are not prepared, students might miss out, or it could impact your ongoing program and preparation in other areas. If you are prepared, your students could enjoy some unique learning and hopefully create some great memories as well. It could also mean that you've extended the opportunity to students' families, wider community and possibly even enhanced relationships with your colleagues. Best of all on these special days, when you have everything sorted out – you get to have a fun day, too!

Short-term planning

Short-term planning focuses your everyday routine on what is happening daily as well as over the coming days or weeks.

Information wall

A space in the classroom that is easy to access, but slightly out of the way of student use, is a beneficial area to dedicate to classroom organisation and information. This is useful for yourself and for any other teacher who might be working in that space (for example, the release teacher or a casual covering you for the day). This is a space where you can display the following:

- Playground duty roster with your duties highlighted
- Classroom schedule for the week
- Support timetable
- Timeslots where students are withdrawn
- Term calendar of events, for example, assembly

This is not a space for confidential information such as Individual Education Plans. Check with your supervisor if this place is suitable for evacuation or lockdown information, as this usually needs to be accessible near exit points for safety reasons.

Relief teacher

There will be times when a casual or relief teacher will need to take your class, whether it's planned or unexpected. This could be if you are sick or are off-site for professional learning. Having the following systems will assist that teacher in keeping structure and consistency for the class – even for a teacher that already knows the class well. If the school does not have a system in place for this, I recommend making your own relief teacher booklet to assist them with the day, including these things:

- Brief welcome note with a blurb about your class environment and any particular notes, for example, *'Please feel free to use the class computers, but please don't use the craft supplies in the bottom cupboard'*
- Class timetable/schedule
- Roster of daily support, withdrawal, intervention
- Class profile with some information about additional needs – if there are high needs that require more information for the teacher, mark their name with an asterisk with a note to see your supervisor before starting class for the day
- Map of the school, including evacuation and lockdown procedures – note where in the classroom these are already displayed along with any relevant medical information about students with needs
- School or class expectations for behaviour and any relevant processes associated with it
- Curriculum information for the term, for example, *'This term in science, we are learning about forces'*
- A list of what books are OK for the teacher to use, for example, *'Please feel free to have students complete work in their workbook, maths book and spelling book'*
- Template for recording the information for the class for the day – either prewritten by you for the teacher to follow or one for them to record and provide to you

Relief teacher template

Daily Schedule

| Casual teacher: | Replacing: | Class: | Date: |

8:30–8:55am	Before school – please check noticeboard in staffroom for changes
9–10:15am	**Roll** **First session**
10:15–11:20am	**Fruit break** **Second session**
11:20–12:10pm	Lunch
12:10–1:40pm	**Middle session** **Warm-up game**
Recess	
2–3pm	**Afternoon session**

| Timeout support class: | Executive support: |

Thank you for taking the class today.

Completed relief teacher – example

Daily Schedule

Casual teacher: Monika	Replacing: Rebecca	Class: 2 Topaz	Date: 30/8/17

8:30–8:55am	Before school – please check noticeboard in staffroom for changes
9–10:15am	**Roll** – ask students to read their familiar readers (in the red box) for 10 minutes. **Guided reading groups** – activities are at the back cupboard. The students can help put them out on the tables. Students can move around the activities at their own choice, including Google Classroom (only the students who haven't done their D&D character sheet). Please read with Max (on his own) and Oliver and Liam together – if he will read. When finished, please make sure students pack up properly and put resources in the back cupboard neatly.
10:15–11:20am	**Fruit break** – please read a story from the whiteboard while students eat their fruit. **Writing** – join with the class next door for the writing session. The class teacher is expecting you and will have everything. Please support her with the class. Students Isabella, William, Emma and Ben will need the most support.
11:20–12:10pm	Lunch & first play break
12:10–1:40pm	**Maths:** **Warm-up game** – students play 'Addition Wars'. They have played it a few times this week and know how to play. Ask them to show you how to play as practice, then they can get into small groups to play (cards are at the bottom of the whiteboard). **Word problem** – (students will need some support for this) Write the problem on the board and have children identify the important parts and words. *Calvin read his book for 3 minutes every night for a week. Hobbes read his book for 5 minutes every night. How much more time did Hobbes spend reading his book compared to Calvin last week?* Then write this up and go through this – talk about how it is more open-ended. Students can copy this problem into their maths book (with short date and a title): *Calvin read his book for 3 minutes every night for a week. Hobbes read his book for 5 minutes every night.* *The answers are 35, 2, 21, 56, 14. What might the questions be?* **Maths games** – there are maths games in the storeroom on the left on the bottom shelf. Students can play those if there is extra time.
Recess	
2–3pm	**Science** – in the back of Science books (in tray on back shelf), ask students to write their own description for how to make a paper airplane (they followed instructions to make one yesterday). Write up on the whiteboard an example of the steps and include pictures of the paper folding. Ask them how they followed the steps and what made it easy or hard to understand in the instructions they used yesterday. Make sure you remind students to use neat writing and to take care when drawing their pictures.

Timeout support class: *2 Quartz*	Executive support: *Ms Ayad (Principal)*

Thank you for taking the class today. You will see that Max doesn't work independently. The SLSO Maya will come and take him to read, but when he comes in the room you will need to make him sit at an activity and ask a student to help him. (He has activities in his silver folder on his desk but needs help with most of it.) Wei or James work well with him. They are a very fun class that respond best to positive reinforcement, praise and humour. Feel free to give them as many Dojo Points as you like and remind them they have a reward on Friday if they continue doing the right thing.

Thanks! Bec ☺

Daybook

I highly recommend using a daybook in the form of a printed or digital planner. Even though I prefer to program digitally, my personal preference for a daybook is printed with a week across two pages so I can open my daybook and see the week ahead. The one I use also has sections for appointments, to-do lists, priority lists and includes the weekend. This is helpful so I know if there is something important happening on the weekend and I need time to prepare for it during the week. There are many companies that make these specifically for teachers and include things like stickers for reminders, Post-it notes and often include relevant information such as the teaching standards, wellbeing activities, etc. It pays to shop around and find a company that has already created a template with a style you think will work for you.

Your daybook is a good place to map out school events, staff administration meetings, professional learning sessions and upcoming personal days where you know you will need to take a day off. This will help you take note of any impact that will occur to your class, your programming, any scheduling conflicts and if you need to prepare anything for meetings or communication. Utilise the to-do list and look ahead at the next couple of weeks. Note down things that are due soon, so it's not left to the last minute. This could be deadlines for the assessment schedule, academic reports, parent-teacher meetings or tasks pertaining to professional learning.

Example from my daybook – from Createl Publishing

Resources

Look ahead in your program for the upcoming two to three weeks to see what resources you may need in lesson prep. In the best circumstances, these will be available in your school somewhere and you will only need to coordinate borrowing the materials. If this is something pertinent to your whole teaching team, then coordinate with them during team meetings to check who will need what materials and when they are needed. If these need to be borrowed out, make sure there is a plan for who will borrow them for the team and when, as well as who will return them and when. For example, if the whole team is teaching a measurement task that requires borrowing the scales and weights from the maths storeroom, check your class timetables and lessons to ensure there are enough materials to be shared across the team. If not, then you will need to coordinate how and when the materials will be moved between the classrooms in that time. Never leave this to the last minute or you might find resources have already been borrowed by another grade and you will need to plan for something else with little notice.

Always check in school storerooms on the quality and quantity of materials well before you are due to teach with them. For various reasons, you will find materials are damaged or missing and this has gone unreported to the people who manage the borrowing system. If you find something damaged or missing, please report it as soon as possible. It's very helpful in keeping resources up to date. If something gets damaged or lost while borrowed by you, please don't return it that way. We're all human and are allowed to make mistakes – as are our students. If a student has damaged something from misuse, follow your school policy to manage the behaviour.

If you need materials for learning that aren't available in the school, communicate this with your supervisor to see if it is something the school can purchase before spending your own money – unless you want to own the resource. School leadership needs to be aware if resources aren't available in the school and use this information to plan for the school budget and future needs. This may also mean updating programs with current resource needs.

Student routines

There will be routines in your class that work best if the students are part of the process – yes, even in the youngest grades. With explicit teaching and guidance, students can support the positive and effective flow of the day and the regular routines. This will mean taking the time in the day for teaching these routines and making sure you don't skip steps in the process. It is well worth taking the time to do this, as your class will settle into the class schedule and build a teamwork atmosphere. There will be students with alternate needs that could be supported using visuals or multi-step instructions when learning these routines and expectations.

An example of this is borrowing books from the library. Work with the school librarian or staff involved in coordinating the library space to learn the procedures and routines. Dedicate time to explicitly teaching the students where everything is in the library and the borrowing system to be used. Things like where to line up, how to hold the book with the barcode out to packing library books in their bag, where to where to return books, etc. These things may seem like small things, but when you have a class of 30 students all doing different things and asking questions about what to do, it will take up a lot of your library session – and that time is highly valuable.

The same applies in your own classroom. Think of the way you would like student books to be handed out. By you or by student monitors? How does work get collected? Who will collect the lunch orders from the canteen? Will you turn on class computers in the morning so they are ready to use, or will you have a student turn them on to start the day?

I highly recommend a class task chart for these things, and rotating names in the chart every week. Consider students who might have anxiety with these tasks or if any students potentially need support to participate. If students have high needs, do not exclude them from this opportunity – design support options that will allow them to engage along with their peers. This will also help build responsibility within the task and allow students to take ownership of the learning in the classroom.

Long-term planning

Long-term planning focuses on mapping out for future programs, activities and special events. Planning for the long term will support a good balance between personal and professional life.

School calendar

There will likely be an official school calendar where activities and events are recorded to allow for planning and preparation. Most schools now have a digital platform with online access to enable you to check dates and times at school or from off-site. Make sure you check with your supervisor what the process is for adding information to this calendar, or if you need to request a variation to routine, especially if you are a member of a committee organising anything that requires booking dates or making staff aware of changes to the school routine. Even if this is something at the end of the year, once you know your preferred date, book it in the school calendar. This will support your colleagues on other committees to not clash with events and to make sure that certain weeks aren't overloaded with variations to routine.

When it comes to programming and planning for your own class, look ahead at the entire term or semester of events and activities to allow you to work around anything that will impact your class. Some events might last for an hour, while others might run the entire day. If your class is missing a whole day of your planned curriculum, you will need to take this into account and modify your planning to ensure students don't miss pertinent lessons. Many school events support the curriculum, and you can plan for them, for example, sports carnivals, musical concerts and excursions.

If something impacts your release time from class, ensure you communicate with your supervisor to navigate how this time will be reimbursed to you in a timely manner. The most likely thing to cause this would be a school excursion or event where certain dates were the only option. With forward planning and clear communication, this can usually be accommodated to suit all involved.

Academic reporting

Academic reporting occurs at least twice per year – usually once per semester – and schools design their own schedule for when they are provided to parents and carers. Some schools will design a timeline for reporting to ensure an appropriate time frame for assessment to occur and inform the reports. It is important you align your assessment schedule with your program and allow time for writing reports based on evidence of learning in your classroom.

You will use formative and summative assessment as well as your classroom observations to write these reports. Reports take time. Some teachers prefer to write a whole report for one student for every subject and then move on to the next student. Some teachers prefer to write all the student comments for one subject and then move on to the next subject. There is no best way to do this, only what works best for you and the scheduling expectations of your school. Make sure you schedule breaks for yourself, too.

For more on report writing, check out the following:

www.youtube.com/watch?v=luQ0lh_TNQ4

www.youtube.com/watch?v=zDQZ_x9goO4

Report timeline – example

Due dates	Report schedule tasks	My to-do list
Holidays		Effort scores all KLAs
Week 1		Comments for PDHPE, Sci & Tech, CA
Week 2		Maths comments
Week 3		English comments
Monday **Week 4**	Set up Academic Reporting Period online	Proofread all KLAs and edit where needed. Check comments against achievement scores
Monday **Week 6**	Comments and grades to supervisors	Hand into supervisor. Make necessary edits
Monday **Week 8**	Completed reports due to supervisors	
Friday **Week 8**	Attendance data imported onto reports by executive	
Tuesday **Week 9**	Reports printed by admin staff (back-up day Thursday)	Sign reports
Monday **Week 10**	REPORTS GO HOME	Hand out to students. Absent reports to office

Transition activities/events

Transitioning to a new junction in learning is often compiled of many exciting activities and events. These can often occur at the end of the year and can be planned ahead to avoid overlapping with others and supports a less chaotic workload for the end of the year. These events include transition to early childhood, primary school, high school and higher education.

Many schools run multiple sessions for orientation to a new school setting and this can last for an hour or the whole day. If you are coordinating these sessions, it is important to have these dates and times mapped out as early as possible and communicated across the school with any other teams doing the same thing. For example, anyone coordinating Kindergarten transition to communicate with teachers on Year 6 to make sure it doesn't clash with their dates for transition to high school. They may not have anything to do with each other's events, but it reduces the complications for the whole school to not have too many events happening on the same day. Consider if there is an emergency that day and how many staff might not be on-site if there are too many events occurring. Or how many parents will be calling the office to clarify information all calling on the same morning. Sometimes these complexities cannot be predicted, but the open communication between all involved will support a clear pathway of planning for everyone. This will also support families who have siblings attending both events/activities.

End-of-year activities

End-of-year activities are usually celebrations and often an annual event where the organisation doesn't necessarily need to change much from year to year. This can include presentation/awards ceremonies, rewards days, farewells, graduation assemblies, etc. The key to planning ahead for these is to get started in Term 1, especially for the graduations and farewells. Those dates need to be booked well in advance and often require a deposit paid by a certain time. Don't delay on things like this. These can creep up on you and before you know it, you become snowed under by report writing and end-of-year assessments on top of it all.

Tip 4 summary

- Have information ready to access in the classroom.

- Ensure a relief teacher has easy access to class information and can communicate about the day.

- Utilise a daybook (printed or digital) to stay on top of daily planning, special events and upcoming items.

- Plan ahead for the use of resources and communicate with your team if needing to share or borrow anything.

- Explicitly teach students the routines and expectations in class management, including organisation that does not only occur inside your classroom.

- Use the school calendar and check it as part of your regular practice – if you are organising anything in the school, then ensure you use the school calendar to make others aware of what is happening across the school.

- Prepare for report writing by using a timeline to space out your workload, align with other programming/assessment expectations and adhere to school report writing deadlines.

- Be mindful of end-of-year activities or events and ensure these are planned for early in the year to avoid clashes, conflicts or communication issues with colleagues, students and parents.

Tip 5

Monitor your workload

Many people will often say that the best organisational skill you can have is effective time management. Time management is an important part of being a teacher and it's a skill that will benefit you throughout your career. I think it's important that prior to developing quality use and allocation of time, you learn how to prioritise your tasks and work habits most effectively.

What has become increasingly evident in most recent years is the additional load that has been placed in the laps of teachers and educational leaders, without the removal of other roles or responsibilities. This is on top of the high expectations of educators and the goals we set for ourselves to be the best teachers we can be.

Teachers have often been showcased in the media, and other political outlets, in a manner that is negative and patronising, which has led to teachers feeling the need to take on an excessive workload to compensate for the stereotype being played out. It can take a long time to recognise the need and benefits of a good life-work balance. It is imperative that you consciously refine these skills and monitor your workload and wellbeing before a serious mental – or physical – issue forces you to adopt healthier habits in either your personal or professional life.

Some teachers in their early years have expressed the pressure they have felt to take on an additional load to either prove themselves or maintain consistent work if they are not employed permanently. Some teachers take on an additional load because they are excited and eager to be teaching. As every person is different, they will balance these loads differently. Take time to monitor if your behaviours are being impacted. Are you less patient, more tired, skipping personal hobbies, etc? If so, you might be taking on too much at work.

Additional workload

What do I mean when I refer to 'additional workload'? These are roles or responsibilities undertaken in addition to the mandatory requirements of your role as a classroom teacher. These are things that will extend you beyond the needs of your class and your requirements to plan, assess and report on student learning.

They may include:

- Extracurricular:
    - Choir/dance/drama/band
    - Sports/e-sports
    - Boardgames, for example, chess, checkers
    - Lego/STEM
    - Student leadership team
    - Crafting, for example, knitting, sewing
    - Building, for example, model plane or car kits

- Committees:
    - Curriculum (Key Learning Areas)
    - Behaviour
    - Engagement
    - Community
    - Culture
    - School targets
    - Attendance
    - Learning Support Team

- Clubs:
    - Social
    - Wellbeing
    - Fitness
    - Teams/school initiatives

- Special events (Religious, cultural, Book Week, etc):
    - Newsletter
    - Fundraising

And many more, depending on your school culture and context.

Prioritising class and additional roles

The priority of what you do in your teaching load will vary throughout the year. Each term brings different events, teaching areas and assessments. If you are taking on extracurricular additional loads, these may have various requirements for your time and effort that could change across the school year. For example, the sports team might only play for one term, whereas the choir may have multiple performances throughout the year. The sports teams might need coaching before or after school. The chess club might only be able to meet at lunch breaks.

Before volunteering for extracurricular activities, be mindful of the additional time for the activities involved, any personal time you might need to contribute and what preparation work you will need time for. Ask for clarification on what will be expected from you before you take on the additional load, and what the goal of the initiative is. Some initiatives are strategically linked to enhance student learning, while some are for engagement and wellbeing. Some are funded by schools or grants donated to the school. While all the activities offered to students will have some level of value, there might be certain ones that require a higher level of time and dedication. Find out as much as you can before agreeing to this addition to your workload. This will allow you to prioritise your time and your effort with a clear set of expectations.

Over the page is an example of how you might shift priorities across the term, or work with another colleague to share the responsibilities.

Priorities shift template

	Class	Choir	Notes
Week 1		Prep for open day	
Week 2	Open day	Open day	
Week 3			
Week 4	Reading data	No rehearsal	(or Mrs White run)
Week 5	Running assembly	Longer rehearsal	
Week 6	Maths data	No rehearsal	(or Mrs White run)
Week 7			
Week 8	Reports due		
Week 9		2 rehearsals to prep for performance	Mrs White to take 2nd rehearsal
Week 10		Performance	

The mandatory vs the 'extra'

Teaching is an industry filled with people who greatly value how important our role is as educators of young people and this sometimes fuels us to stretch ourselves too far. We know how much our students benefit from it and focus on what they might be missing out on if we don't go above and beyond. You only have to search online for pictures of classrooms to see the hours, energy, time and money that has gone into transforming a classroom into a wonderland of engagement and opportunity. There is no shame in going above and beyond to create this space. There is also no shame in setting boundaries for yourself to ensure you don't stretch yourself so far that it becomes detrimental.

Learning spaces can indeed be enhanced by those visually appealing aspects of the physical environment. Learning will also be enhanced if your energy is spent on building a quality learning culture in that learning space. Reflect on what is valuable to your teaching practice and what is best for your students. This helps prioritise the value of where your time and energy are best directed for your class – and don't feel guilty about a well-informed choice.

The same approach can be utilised when it comes to administrative load. Teachers have mandatory programming requirements based on the governing body in their state or their employer. These are not negotiable and must be prioritised. There are ways to ensure you meet your requirements without adding excessive work to your admin load. Cooperative or collaborative programming shares the load among colleagues. Many employers offer units of work as samples or guides. Curriculum across the nation and within states also share examples and guides for all grades and subjects. These may not be the highest-quality documents, or the most recent, but they may help you during a time when priorities are becoming a challenge. If a teaching unit is a high priority in a short amount of time and you are unsure where to begin, or what a unit should consist of, look to your colleagues for support – whether they are in your team, your school or in the wider professional network of colleagues. Many teachers share great programs freely.

The hard days

There will be times throughout the school year when work becomes cumbersome. The priorities will get muddled, the load will become heavy and everything hits at the same time no matter how much you tried to plan in advance. Teachers are generally very good at being resilient, flexible and getting on with whatever comes their way. Sometimes we do this for too long, and that's when burnout can begin. This can happen for our students, too. When too much is going on at home and too much is going on at school, everything just becomes too hard. Everything. That's OK. It's normal and we all feel it at one time or another. It's hard to tell sometimes, though. Teachers are very good at putting on a brave face and getting on with the day.

When days get hard like this, remember who your support network is. This can be your team, supervisor, other colleagues in the school or network, people you studied with, your friends or your family. In more serious situations, always seek professional help to ensure you are caring for your mental and physical health. When I was an early career teacher, I would fight those hard days. I would keep trying to bring it back into line: I would make continual adjustments, change the routine or even move the class to a different space in the school. Some days it worked. Other days I just needed to accept it was a hard day and there was absolutely nothing I could do about it. We can't fix everything.

Don't take those bad days too personally. Sometimes we stuff up. Oftentimes, it's out of our control. Sometimes we just didn't plan ahead and it didn't work out. It happens, and it's fine. We learn from it, and grow, and use that knowledge to do it a bit differently next time. It does not mean you are a bad teacher. It does not mean you are a bad person. We're all human and you don't have to prove yourself.

> **"This is just a moment in time,
> step aside and let it happen".**
>
> – Inara Serra *(Firefly)*

Life-work balance

Read that title again. Life-work, not work-life. Life comes first – and don't forget it. Me being a Xennial – microgeneration between GenX and Millennial – means I grew up with the expectation that you must give your employer 110%, show up early, stay late, take on all the extra roles and don't call in sick (it's a sign of weakness apparently). I grew up being instilled with the notion that you don't say no to your boss. Even if it was something you didn't know how to do. You say yes and figure out a way to get it done.

However, in teaching, that doesn't seem to be just a generational factor. Teachers sometimes find it hard to say no to things we know will be great for the students. Even if it means staying back late, losing sleep or spending personal money.

"Oh, this term your class is reading *The Lion, the Witch and the Wardrobe*, that's so cool. You should design a wardrobe for your classroom door so the kids can walk into Narnia every morning when they start school!" Far out, Susan, yes that sounds like an amazing idea! But I don't have anything I can use for that. I would need to buy all the materials, spend the weekend painting it (because we start reading next week and it would be a great way to start the book), then I need to come in on Sunday to install it.

This sounds so cool I even have a hard time writing the word 'no' to this. But you can say no. You can acknowledge that you already have a lot on this weekend. That you're saving for a family holiday and don't want to impact that plan. And really, the students will still enjoy the book just as much without the magical classroom doors. Perhaps it could become a class art project instead of something that takes up your budget and your weekend. That way it's more meaningful for the students and you can maintain a healthier life-work balance, keeping your weekend for yourself.

I want you to think of this question when you're unsure if a task or responsibility might create a negative life-work imbalance:

Is this an actual or just a perceived detriment to the students?

Imagining the benefit to students in your mind and deciding not to do it is not the same thing as actually taking something away from the students.

Reflection and feedback

You will have many opportunities in your teaching career to engage in conversations with your supervisor relating to your teaching capabilities and goals for the future. These can be great opportunities to be open and honest about the good, the bad and the ugly. Sometimes these conversations can be challenging. For both you and your supervisor. Early in your career you might think you need to take this head-on yourself, but you don't. If these conversations are difficult to manage, please seek out a trusted colleague or peer to support you through those conversations. You have that right and it is not a judgement if you ask for support.

I mention this because these moments can blur your workload. Things that seemed important before may not seem important after a challenging conversation. Continue to reflect on your values, your roles and responsibilities, the difference between mandatory and extra and, of course, your life-work balance. If you need a break, take a break. Breathe and review where needed. If you need to take a step back from any of that additional load, be honest and take the break. Sometimes those extra roles are what keep us happy at work. In which case, don't give it up, just keep monitoring your workload.

Tip 5 summary

- Be aware of the time, energy, responsibilities and expectations involved in extracurricular roles.

- Manage the classroom load with any additional roles by prioritising tasks and timelines, and share loads with peers.

- Know what your mandatory requirements are and what is extra. Schools will sometimes have their own internal expectations that are not necessarily mandatory requirements of the job. Know the difference.

- Embrace the hard days. You will learn from them.

- Maintain a healthy life-work balance by monitoring how often you say yes to things, and if you ever say no.

- Utilise reflection and feedback from others as a way to check and monitor if there is a workload issue.

Tip 6

Proactively build relationships

Relationships come first. Without building genuinely positive relationships with students, teachers, parents and community, you are limiting your chances of making a significant, positive impact in someone's education – or even their life. You can be the most enthusiastic, positive, engaging teacher in the world, and those kids won't absorb as much as they would if they believe they had a genuine connection to you, and know that you believe in them.

The benefits of making and sustaining these relationships go much deeper than enhancing student outcomes. Extending these connections to parents and the community will provide you with deep insight to the lives of your students and how to best meet their social and emotional needs, and how to support their wellbeing while engaging them in the best learning opportunities possible. Even students in affluent areas need support when things aren't structured well at home, or when life brings about significant change. Parents will highly value your role as the teacher of their child(ren) when you make the effort to build a rapport with them. Sometimes the relationship between school and home can take time to develop, and whatever effort you make in this will benefit the student as they continue with their education.

Relationships with colleagues can be much like those you might experience with your family. Some you are close with, and others you avoid like pineapple on pizza (actually, I like pineapple on pizza – but I'm sure you get the drift). Unfortunately, there might be some you just don't get along with. It's important that you focus on the positive relationships and make sure you reflect consistently to ensure you're not contributing to chaos. I believe it's worth being vulnerable with colleagues once you develop enough trust to do so.

Implement restorative practices

In the first years of teaching, this can easily be confused with trying to be a friend with your students. You cannot be a friend with a student – you can be kind and caring, but not a friend. The distinction needs to be very clear for yourself and for your students. It is important to set this boundary, both for yourself and for the students. Especially as students are still learning the social skills and behaviours that are appropriate between children and adults.

Engaging effectively with students relies heavily on consistent practices. If kids know what your expectations are and that your responses will be generally consistent, then they will be more likely to respond to the methods you put in place. If you are inconsistent, then students won't accurately reflect on the expectations, and they may not value your responses as the teacher.

I recommend implementing positive reinforcement practices, and not focus on negative consequences. Consequences can be positive, but many children are not familiar with a positive consequence as a concept. If you choose to use that type of language, ensure you explicitly teach it first. There will be times when consequences are warranted, which can depend on the school system in which you teach. Schools will often have a whole-school system for behavioural expectations and consequences that needs to be used in the classroom. This should not prevent you from implementing your own style of management in the classroom that suits your class needs. You can enhance school-wide practices by using methods that suit you and cater for your class. Be confident to share strategies that work with your supervisor or colleagues. Sometimes changes are needed to keep practices relevant or current.

Some students with additional needs will need individualised behaviour management strategies. Sometimes it's easy to connect these strategies to school practices and other times it will need to be heavily modified. These modifications and strategies all need to be documented. I highly recommend you take the time to invest in quality professional learning about restorative practices and encourage your colleagues to do the same. It works best as a whole-school practice.

Staff

It doesn't matter if your school is big or small, there will be staff you connect well with, and you may even have a work bestie. But there will also be staff you don't connect well with. Some you possibly clash with. I wish I could tell you that teachers know better than to gossip or bully, but unfortunately teachers are humans, too. And humans are not without fault. If you haven't engaged in any kind of learning about emotional intelligence, now might be a good time to tread the waters in that topic. Sometimes those tough students are easy in comparison to working alongside a difficult colleague. And that, my new graduates, is a fact of life. But don't let it get you down. For every challenging colleague, I'm confident you will find five, 10, 20 colleagues to lift you up, cheer you on and share in the love of teaching and learning.

Consider when you begin teaching that a school staff is not just made up of teachers. There are:

- **Facilities** – first and foremost these staff keep our schools functioning – general assistants and cleaners
- **Executive** – the leadership team, such as Assistant Principal, Head Teacher, Deputy Principal and Principal
- **Administration** – Business Manager, Administration Manager, Administration Officer, clerks, etc
- **Teachers** – class teachers, support teachers, specialist teachers, language teachers, etc

- **Specialists** – speech pathologist, occupational therapist, school psychologist/counsellor, physio, school nurse, etc
- **Additional educators** – School Learning Support Officers (also known as teacher aides), Aboriginal Education Officers, etc
- **Itinerant/regional staff** – Student Engagement Officer, Home School Liaison Officer, behaviour specialist, hearing specialist, etc

This is not everyone! Schools are complex systems, with many people working together to ensure kids can access quality education.

Parents

Regardless of where you teach, parents will bring their own attitude or opinion based on their own school experiences. This can be focused on education overall, teaching practices or learning in general. Some parents have expectations for their children to experience school as they had. If they are my age, they would be expecting tables in rows, sometimes groups, all facing the board with lots of bookwork based on what was written on the chalkboard. I'm glad my kids didn't have the same experience I did. Not that my schooling was bad, but those methods have been improved. And I want my kids to have access to all the new and improved things – if they enjoy it and learn from it.

If you are a new (and young) graduate, chances are you have had the chance to experience more current educational practices and may have some challenges in helping older parents understand the 'new and improved shiny things' in the classroom. That's OK, because really the most it takes to build a connection with parents is listening and acknowledging their perspective and communicating openly with them to help them understand. Keep that in your mind any time you are trying to build a relationship with a parent or carer – listen and acknowledge.

For example, consider this scenario:

> John's mother comes to the class teacher and seems anxious about John working in a small group with the teacher during writing lessons. She says, "I don't want other kids thinking he's stupid and

can't write by himself." Instead of explaining straight away what the reason is for the small-group teaching, the teacher asks John's mother why she believes the other kids would think that of John. His mother explains: "When I was at school, only the low kids would work in small groups with the teacher, while everyone else just did class work at their table. So, if you were with the teacher, everyone saw you as dumb." This personal perspective allows the teacher the chance to empathise with John's mother and acknowledge her experience was a difficult one. The teacher can then take the opportunity to describe current practices in targeted teaching and how these structures are used across the whole class in all learning areas.

External support agencies

There are numerous agencies working across the country to support students to engage with education. These can be accessed by parents through a self-referral or a referral supported by the school. They are voluntary and parents can be supported on a short-term or long-term basis. These services will identify goals and targets based on the needs of the family, and if they involve school, then they will engage with the school through appropriate channels. This may be through your principal, another executive or the learning support team coordinator.

Some examples of these agencies include:

- Benevolent Society
- Catholic Care
- Uniting
- Barnardos

Families will have a caseworker to support their engagement in the program and this will be the person you can connect with to ensure the best possible outcomes for the children and the family. Sometimes this support can involve confidential and sensitive information. It is vital that this type of information remains that way and that you do not divulge any additional information you may have previously been unaware of to your colleagues that are not involved in the support process. Ensure you always follow mandatory reporting procedures as necessary.

Sometimes working with families that have high additional support needs can be challenging, especially if you have not experienced a home life with similar complexities. Conversations and details can be confronting, and I highly recommend seeking support if you find the situation to be difficult. The school counsellor is a good example of a colleague who can share some strategies they use when separating home life and work life. Otherwise, utilise mental health days when you need them or please seek professional medical advice to support you appropriately.

Community

No two communities are the same. And this is a good thing. I love the diversity that can be found in communities around schools – even in small ones. Your community can be your biggest ally and supporter if you work together towards common goals. I feel like I can guarantee you there is some small business out there that really wants to give back to the community in some way. Perhaps they can't help financially, but they would love to come and help cook snags for a sausage sizzle fundraiser and get a little shoutout in the school newsletter for contributing.

There are bigger businesses that have community liaison officers to focus on community partnerships and would love an invitation to contribute to school projects. Bunnings helps build frog ponds; Woolworths donates gift cards; and local bakeries donate cakes for fundraisers. They are well worth taking the time to say hi. And, of course, don't forget to meet with your Parents & Community (P&C) and your local Aboriginal Educational Consultancy Group (AECG) Inc.

Tip 6 summary

- Proactively build relationships using restorative practices that use positive reinforcement, not just consequences.

- Build language around restorative practices with students and also with staff across the school.

- Encourage the use of school-wide restorative practices.

- There are different types of staff in a school, and they all play a vital role in ensuring a school is a great place to learn. Get to know their names, value what they bring to the school and treat their role with respect.

- Parents have their own experiences and expectations of what school is or should be. Listen to and acknowledge parents and carers to work towards a common goal.

- External agencies can become a big role in your student's life and wellbeing. Your support helps them.

- Support your local community! Shop with them, join local events and get them involved wherever you can.

Tip 7

Set clear and explicit expectations

The behaviour of students has often been reported to me as one of the hardest things that a new teacher has to manage. It can entirely depend on the systems set within the school and the whole-school expectations for student behaviour. These systems reflect the values of the school and the practices being used by the teachers to reinforce those values. If a school has very clear expectations and values, these are important to reiterate and utilise within your class, while also bringing attention to areas of focus that are particular to your class needs. If there is not something from the school, then use this chance to develop something tailored to your class.

Behaviours in a class can adapt and change based on the factors influencing students' day. You may have a class with high absences and those students don't receive your regular reinforcement of values and expectations. You may have a class with high attendance; however, there may be a large number of students with language barriers that need additional supports to be able to learn, understand and enact the values and expectations within the school or classroom. Therefore, regardless of student background or need, your expectations for students must be clear and explicit.

When I say clear and explicit, I mean broken down into necessary steps, explained in detail, posed in scenarios, visuals on the wall and students can repeat these to you with an understanding of what they need to do as students to meet those values and expectations. It's one thing to have a poster on your wall saying: *Be Safe*, but what does 'safe' mean to each student in that room? 'Safe' for a child fleeing a war-torn nation as a refugee means something very different to a child who has always slept soundly in their own bed with a full belly of dinner and dessert.

Set expectations early and reinforce regularly

Setting expectations begins on the first day with your class. You set it in the first way you interact with your students. There used to be a ridiculous old-school mentality that a teacher shouldn't smile in their classroom until Easter, that being stern would get the kids in line and you wouldn't have any issues with behaviour all year. I don't recommend the strategy. A smile can go a long way for a child. As can a high-five, a fist bump or even the thumbs-up.

Starting early with expectations can begin with a conversation or delving into some deep lessons. I recommend spreading that over the first two weeks and allocating time to it. Some may view this as 'not real learning', but it's definitely important learning that will enable your class to engage in the learning to come, and provide some base skills needed to continue through their schooling and even into life beyond school. Even in the workplace we have expectations for our behaviour and conduct.

These early lessons can take the school expectations, or rules, and be split up into sections for each day and allow the students to participate in open dialogue about their interpretation of the expectation/rule and create some support resources for the classroom. This might be posters, images or even videos of what it looks like in practice. Teachers can use examples as a guide, but then have the students create something that is their design and have some ownership about the expectations in the classroom.

Reinforcement of values and expectations must happen regularly. Behaviour will slide over the year when they are not upheld clearly and explicitly. This can be with refresher lessons each term. When you do it will depend on your class. Some teachers like to do it at the beginning of each term, and some like to revisit midterm as a preventative measure for when students get a bit tired and overwhelmed at the end of the term. When you plan for these reinforcement sessions, this is an opportunity to revise any resources made at the beginning of the year. The students might have developed some new vocabulary that would be beneficial in any posters made or situations that they can reflect on.

Support materials

Support materials for school expectations might be provided for each class with requirements for how or where they are displayed in the room. For example, there might be a poster of school rules with the requirement it is placed near the front board in the classroom. I recommend following this school provision, as it supports consistency and routine for all your students. They will know that, regardless of what classroom they are in or which teacher they have, the expectations across the school remain the same.

Following the school provisions should not preclude you from enhancing student learning about the school expectations with your own materials to support student understanding. If you work in a school where there is a high number of students where English is not their first language, then there will be a huge benefit to adding images as a visual support to understand the expectation. Schools may include language translations if they have many students new to the country. Sometimes this might also include images of what is inappropriate with a line or cross through the image, so students with high language barriers can interpret and understand what the expectation means in a variety of contexts. You can imagine it might be hard for a student with minimal English-speaking skills to understand that in the STEM lab it's OK to draw on the desks because they are whiteboard surfaces, but it's not OK to draw on the desks in the classroom, which are not whiteboard surfaces.

Videos are a great resource for developing student understanding about behaviours – even for adults this can be a complex thing to discuss. Seeing a behaviour-specific scenario on the screen can include guiding information such as lighting, music or even narration. It frees you up as a teacher to then follow up and ask hard-hitting questions like: "What would you have done in this situation?", "How could this problem have been avoided?" or "What would have been a good way to have this conversation?" Using video resources (there are many on YouTube) helps avoid the students worrying that a scenario you use is specifically about them. When students make their own video examples, it's highly valuable for all.

Incentives and consequences

There are many opinions among teachers about what is or isn't effective to use for student behaviour. There are schools that have explicit procedures for incentives and consequences across the school, while there are other schools where teachers are given guides and can create their own class systems. I've experienced both styles, and there are downsides and benefits to any system in place. The best you can do as a class teacher is find the best way to make it work for the students you have in your class each year. Even staying in the same school for many years, it is beneficial to adapt your systems each year to suit the needs of the class.

Incentives might make you think of experiences from your own schooling, or perhaps strategies you saw being used during your practicum placements. There is nothing wrong with utilising an idea that another teacher has used (unless it's something they personalised, then asking consent is the most professional thing to do). I made 'Turner Dollars' in my first year of teaching (Turner is my maiden name). It had my face on it and I matched the paper it was printed on to the colour of Australian money. The kids loved it and got to 'buy' things every Friday from my 'Turner Shop', which had cards for computer time, free time, etc. I've also used table points, individual points, prize boxes and a 'West Winning Wall'.

Over time, I've used many different methods that encourage both extrinsic and intrinsic motivation. Each student has their own version of currency. Some kids will love receiving a stamp with a smiley face, whereas other students really enjoy a sticker. Then there are other kids that don't care about the stamps and stickers, and they do it because you tell them you're proud of them. Others do it because they enjoy it. It all comes down to how well you know your students and building a good rapport with them.

Consequences should never, ever, be the removal of something a student has earned. EVER. Earned is earned. Consequences are a separate system, allowing students the chance to reset and re-engage in learning. This could include break time away from the classroom or meeting with a mentor teacher/executive.

West Winning Wall – a whole-class incentive

A foot was placed on the wall when students successfully had break times without a teacher redirecting negative behaviours. When the six feet reached the top of the wall in that colour, the class would achieve the reward listed at the top of the wall in that colour. And so on through the rest of the colours.

Students with additional behavioural needs

There will be students who require additional support in learning to manage their own behaviours; some might be diagnosed with a specific behavioural need. If a student has been diagnosed, they should have a support plan, sometimes called an Individual Education Plan or Individual

Behaviour Plan – depending on the diagnosis or student needs (see Tip 3 for examples). This can be a complex process involving staff, parents and external specialists. This can be overwhelming when you first experience it. It can involve paperwork, meetings, communication with multiple parties and providing the support to the student in the classroom.

Students with additional behavioural needs may access the school processes for incentives and consequences. Some students may require more specific supports to successfully meet school expectations. This might include a completely different incentive or consequence system targeting specific behavioural needs, or it could be a micro-version of the school-wide systems in place.

For example, a school could use a system of points as an incentive for school expectations. Teachers can award students 10 points at a time for demonstrating the school expectation to 'Be Respectful'. This presents a challenge for a student who has a diagnosis of oppositional defiance disorder and as such has a high degree of difficulty meeting this school expectation, especially on a regular basis. Consistently not meeting this expectation means they are being excluded from opportunities to achieve and receive incentives using the school-wide system. In this case, you can implement the micro-points system – think of it like a coffee card that you get stamped with each coffee before getting a freebie. Then the teacher looks for micro-behaviours that also meet the school expectation, such as saying thank you, or walking in the class without pushing someone, or using appropriate language (these things might be listed goals for that student). The teacher can then reward one point at a time for these behaviours, eventually being able to award the 10 points that other students receive on the school system. This allows them to access the school-wide system, with a personalised approach.

Managing noise

Five years ago, I filmed what is now my most popular video on the Talkin' Chalk YouTube channel. I filmed 'Managing noise in the classroom' after some people had requested it as a topic. It is still a highly requested topic by new teachers, so I just reshare the video and it keeps getting more views. I'll give you some quick tips here, but for the full video you can head to the channel or see the link below.

The key to managing student noise in the classroom is managing your own noise first. This can include your own voice level, playing music in the background or using attention devices like bells or clapping. How you present your own noise will be a guide for what students follow. If you speak loudly, so will they. If you yell across the room to get someone's attention, so will they. If you overuse the attention devices, they will learn to tune them out and the devices will join the background noise.

Sometimes silence is good, sometimes noise is good. There is always a balance between the two and sometimes it can depend on the students you have. I remember I once had a class of students who loved having some music while they worked. They stayed on task and enjoyed taking turns to choose songs. Whereas I had another class who found background music distracting. They weren't calmed by it, but rather heightened by it. Some students found it agitating. Some classes will be a combination of students and in those situations, you can develop some agreements with the class about their noise preferences in the classroom. For example, they may prefer music to only be played during art lessons. It's important as teachers that we respect student preferences.

Managing noise in the classroom

www.youtube.com/watch?v=5m0iGm-jkNw

Playground behaviour

Playground duty can be a fun experience if you're well prepared and maintain consistent expectations. The school expectations should remain the same whether you are in a classroom or in the playground. Know the playground rules and use the same language in conversations with students, utilising the school incentives and consequences. Don't shy away from having those same conversations with students across the school. It can be hard in your first year as you learn student names and, of course, who their siblings and cousins are. Your siblings and cousins are your first friends, so they will engage in conflict with a different level of confidence. This is important as you help them distinguish the difference between conflict at home and conflict at school.

Take notes on behaviour when needed, so you can report it as necessary. Touch base with other students' class teachers to ensure they are aware of a situation before it spills over into the classroom for the next session. My biggest tip of all is: ROAM. Always keep moving and roam when on playground duty and chat to the kids. It's the best preventative measure and helps you get to know the students.

Tip 7 summary

- Set clear and explicit expectations early and reinforce them regularly by revisiting them throughout the year.

- Use a variety of support materials to support student understanding of expectations, such as images, posters, videos or student-created materials that they develop.

- Successful incentives will depend on your class interests and their needs. Try different strategies as needed.

- Students with additional behavioural needs may need a different approach either linked to a current system or might need to be individualised. This can be difficult but well worth it when it is effective and allows for learning.

- Managing your own noise is the key to managing student noise in the classroom. Set the vibe first, then manage.

- Chat to kids and keep roaming during playground duty.

Tip 8

Persevere and reflect on practice

'Pedagogy' is a term used to describe the deep and complex ways in which teaching and learning occur. It's a term that gets used in many ways and scholarly articles will go into detail about the various ways pedagogy can be defined. As a teacher, you will be exposed to different types of pedagogy and your school may adopt specific pedagogies as a whole-school focus.

Education is a process that's constantly changing. The ways in which we teach will also change, as will the ways students learn. Sometimes, they won't change much at all. You will always need to modify and adapt your teaching to suit the needs of your students.

A teaching practice that works with one class may not be as effective with another class. Something that's successful with kindergarten may not be as effective with Year 6. If you type 'Pedagogy' into a Google search, the results will give you enough reading material to last a few years, and by that point new information will be ready for reading as well.

The best way to choose what will work best for your students is to take the time to learn about them and know them well. Develop a deep understanding of their background, culture, family life, socioeconomic status, religion and personal interests. Combine that with quality assessment of learning to determine how to best enhance their education and create engaging, quality learning opportunities. The benefit of pedagogical shifting allows us as educators to be reflective, versatile, lifelong learners. For education to meet the ever-changing needs of our students, so too do teachers need to take time to deeply reflect, adapt and diversify the learning and teaching opportunities and experiences in schools.

Being a reflective practitioner

Being a reflective practitioner can take time and energy out of an already busy day/week/month/year/career. But it's beneficial. I won't quote you from journal articles about the positive impact that can occur when teachers use reflective practices – I don't have the time to write the reference list… I'm a teacher! But that said, I can tell you there are overwhelming examples of research and evidence that supports the practice of reflection and self-awareness. Being reflective will enhance self-awareness and provide you with a personal resolve that allows you to be open to critical feedback, opportunities for growth and development, and allow you to dive deeply into how learning can be enhanced for your students.

Reflections don't need to be an onerous activity. They don't have to be deep and meaningful and occur out in the wilderness, forest bathing under a new moon while Taurus is in retrograde. It can be a quick chat with your neighbour teacher – whether they taught the same lesson as you or not. It can be a couple of dot points under your lesson plans. They can be scribbled or typed. You could record a short video diary and save the video with your program. The point is to take the time to sit back and ask yourself: "So, how did that go? What went well? What would I do differently next time?"

This is not a time to only focus on what can improve; always make sure you note things that went well – even if they feel like small things. These notes you create will either fuel some reinforcement that you're on the right path with your teaching plans or provide an opportunity to stop and shift the plan if needed.

Differentiation

The variety of need within one class can be extensive. Even if it is a class of a singular grade level. The strategies used within classes is entirely dependent on student needs at that point in time. It can be impacted by the resources and staffing available within the school. Differentiation refers to the way in which a teacher modifies or adapts the learning experiences, materials or outcomes to be achieved by the students. One student may have a goal of writing two complex sentences to describe an image, whereas other students in the same class may be working on writing one simple sentence to describe the same image. To support students reaching those different goals, the class teacher may modify the teaching strategy, the writing resources, the instructions and the learning environment, and may group them with other students working towards a similar goal.

Differentiation is a flexible teaching practice that can change daily or over longer periods of time. A teacher may make changes to student groupings for reading sessions every single day, depending on the demonstrated learning and skills covered in lessons from the day before. Alternatively, in writing, the teacher may use a whole-class teaching model for a week and only pull aside certain students for some targeted teaching throughout the week. This approach will shift and change based on the learning intentions of each day and how successfully the students accessed the curriculum and demonstrated independent skills from the task.

Considering how quickly and how often differentiation methods are applied in the classroom across all learning areas, it is understandable that reflection on differentiation can be difficult. If differentiation is needed on the go, the need to document modifications and changes can be time-consuming and impact the energy and availability to take the time needed for a quality reflection. Some suggestions to combat this are to use codes or symbols to account for some reflections, such as thumbs-up/-down, emoji stickers, or a score rating such as a number out of 10. Develop something that's easy for you to interpret or recall when reviewing your teaching practices for that subject and at that point in time.

The revolving door of change

If you have taught for more than 10 years, you will start to feel the pull (or push) of the revolving door that seems to exist within education. It's a door that feels like something you did many years before has come back again. This can be a welcome feeling or bring about emotions filled with dread, depending on what is 'coming back'.

When I started teaching and a new program was being released, for example, a writing or maths program, you would hear the veteran teachers in the back of the meeting room: "We did that one 15 years ago, I thought that they turfed that one!" I used to roll my eyes at those teachers, thinking, "OMG, they are so out of touch, this is such an innovative new program." Now, 20-plus years later, I have realised I have said the same thing so many times after being exposed to some new program or initiative I feel like I've seen many times before. I know now that sometimes this happens when something that worked well before has been rejuvenated to be relevant to current school models and student learning. I also know now that sometimes those teachers who used the program before have some great insights into what worked before and what didn't. Utilise that knowledge and don't be deterred by their frustration – sometimes it can feel very frustrating to be told: "This works – wait, no, stop doing that and do this instead; oh no, wait, go back to the original thing, but add these tweaks." It can feel a bit like a rollercoaster, but you can't see the tracks ahead of the cart.

As a beginning teacher, I encourage you to be the fresh eyes on something that seems to be a resurgence to the more experienced teachers. Ask them for advice and support, team teach together and model for each other. Take that opportunity to reflect together and share insights on what is working and what isn't. Combining reflections between a beginning teacher and an experienced teacher will provide a good range of perspectives on your practice and also allow opportunities to try something new as you modify things. Perseverance is easier when you have someone in the rough with you, trying to do something new or different.

Ever-changing technology

If you are a younger, beginning teacher, then chances are you were born into the age of smart technology. Unless, of course, you are a mid-career entrant, in which case, WELCOME! Your age does not dictate your ability, however, those of us that have been around longer have seen some major changes in technology as we've shifted from vinyl to cassette to CD to iPods and now, we all just stream our music on something like Spotify or iHeartRadio. If you are a younger beginning teacher, you won't know how these technological advances changed the face of education, and how it meant teachers had to adopt and change their practice.

The use of computer labs is pretty much obsolete in most schools and instead we have STEM labs – a place where you will find a multitude of robotics, smart devices with coding apps, green screens, video equipment, podcast microphones, Lego and much more. Moving technology into the classroom has moulded what is in the curriculum and how students can access learning at their point of need. This has allowed school to be more inclusive to students with various communication, language and behavioural needs.

Don't take the technology for advantage. It can absolutely enhance learning for students, but also for your teaching practice. Technology is a tool to keep in your resource and skillset belt, regardless of what grade or subject you teach. I recommend reflecting regularly on what technology you are using, why you are using it and asking yourself some of these questions:

- How does this help my students learn?
- How does this allow students to demonstrate learning?
- How does this support differentiation in my class?
- Are my resources/tools current and relevant?
- Why should I use this technology?
- Who benefits the most from using this technology?
- Is this engaging for my students? Why/why not?
- Are my students technology consumers or creators?
- Am I consuming technology or using it to create?
- Does this learning rely solely on the technology?

Adopting evidence-based pedagogy

The hardest part about reflecting on your teaching and learning practices is understanding and knowing the research and evidence base behind what it is you do, and why it is best for your students. Sometimes, we just get a vibe that something is working well. Sometimes, learning is a long game and you won't see the results of what you have been doing in your class. The teacher they have in three years' time might see the impact, though.

This is why it is important to trust those who spend their days researching and quantifying and qualifying evidence and data to support the development of students and teachers. If you're ever unsure about what this looks like in practice, I recommend continuing your studies. Don't lose touch with academia and the academics who share their knowledge and expertise with us regularly. Study is a reflection tool in itself, and allows many opportunities to persevere.

Tip 8 summary

- Take time to reflect on lessons – informally and formally – by taking notes or records, chatting to your colleagues and making an effort regularly to stop and think.

- Differentiation is a great pedagogy that provides various opportunities to reflect on practice and implement modifications or try something new in your practice.

- Be mindful that education is an industry that is constantly changing and evolving. To keep up with those changes, you need to reflect on practice, be open to new things and work collegially with those around you to ensure you have support, and also that you are a support for others.

- Technology has become a driver of change in many pedagogical practices, so it is important you reflect on your use of technology in the classroom and how it serves your students' learning and development.

- Study and research present current, evidence-based pedagogy for teachers to learn and implement.

Tip 9

Be kind to the relief teacher

Being a casual relief teacher has pros and cons. The varied nature of working on a day-to-day basis means that the positive and negative experiences can change daily – sometimes hourly. This will depend on where they are working and what role they have for the day. It will mainly depend on how prepared they are for a class, and the best way that can happen is when the class teacher provides clear information and has developed structures that support students for when their usual routine changes.

An example of a good casual day is when you get booked well before the workday, some work is provided, the day is well-organised with clearly established routines, students respond well to your expectations, you get a stress-free lunch break, the staff are friendly, you manage to tidy up and write a note before leaving at an appropriate time and you might even get booked for more work.

Then there will be other days that are not so smooth. You will get called in the morning with little notice, there won't be any work left, all the classroom resources will be locked in a cupboard with no key, you'll be allocated a playground duty – which will probably have kids in fights or tears, the class will muck up – right as the principal walks in, the staff won't talk to you during lunch, it will take you well past the expected time to clean up the classroom and write a long note about all the students that had issues during the day and you might not hear of any upcoming work.

Ensuring your class is well-prepared for change demonstrates respect for any teacher in that room for the day, it is a professional courtesy for your fellow colleagues and it will ensure your students have greater potential for a successful day of learning.

Class information

It can be overwhelming for students to have a new face in their learning space. A place that is usually a safe zone can suddenly feel unsafe and scary. By providing the relief teacher with some context for the class can allow the teacher some opportunities to re-establish those safe spaces and even open the door to some relationship building. Never underestimate those small interactions that can be made by knowing some cues to make connections. A student might simply need you to mention that they went fishing on the weekend for one student to suddenly feel safe and connected, because they love fishing with their dad. Another student might need to have an additional five minutes in the morning adjusting to the change in routine. This information is valuable in supporting the relief teacher and your students' ongoing access to learning.

A quick overview of your class could be presented through a tick-box profile (template and example in Tip 3) with some basic information in a one-page overview. More specific information can be shared in a letter (example opposite) and more details for specific student needs added if necessary. Some schools have relief teacher folders with school information such as bell times, school map, playground duty information, etc. If your school does not have this system in place, I recommend making one for your class and made easily accessible to any relief teacher coming into your class, such as your desk or near the most used display space. Alternatively, you could have a space on your information wall specifically for this folder to be kept. As mentioned earlier, share this information with your neighbour teacher, as they might be able to touch base with the relief teacher before classes begin.

The most successful way to prepare for a relief teacher is to ensure your class expectations and procedures are consistent and clear. This could be daily schedules or visuals, class jobs so students know their responsibilities in the classroom and building pride in their learning space. There will be students that test the boundaries, but clear organisation and expectations that are embedded in the classroom are something that are hard to argue with.

Class letter – example

Dear relief teacher,

Thank you for taking my class today. You will be provided with an information folder containing organisation for the school and the class, as well as pertinent information about the students. You will notice I have a slightly smaller class, however, some of the students have high complexities requiring additional support. You might have support staff join the class throughout the day. There may be some learning support officers scheduled to come in and support specific student needs and other teachers will join the class to provide general support to the class. If the identified student they work with is absent, they might have another student to work with, or might support the class in general – or they may need to change their schedule and support a student from another class. When additional staff join the class, please clarify with them what their role is in the class so you are aware of what they will be doing when they join the class. We appreciate your flexibility and understanding that the support staff roles and timetable may change during the day if changes occur. If students are required to leave the classroom, such as an intervention program, please ensure they line up at the door when it is time to go with the messenger and remind them of school expectations to walk quietly, safely and respectfully to their session.

Please don't feel it is a requirement to push through all the work for the day. Having a different teacher can sometimes be overwhelming to this class, so please take the time to ensure students are settled and ready to learn for each session. If this means having a long breathing exercise or brain break, I appreciate you taking the additional time to allow students to settle before engaging in the class work. Students will respond positively when they know you allow them the time they need to be mentally and physically prepared to learn.

Our classroom is located near the toilets, which makes it very easy for students to have quick toilet breaks during class time. We also have sinks nearby for refilling water bottles and students are permitted their water bottles on their desk throughout the day. Please don't allow any other drinks inside the classroom space such as milk or juice, as the whole classroom is carpeted. If the day is very hot, the class will sit at their desk to eat lunch, otherwise there are silver seats just outside the classroom door that students will sit at during eating time.

Our class embeds the use of growth mindset and restorative practices. Any kind of rewards incentive used in the class operates separately to any consequences. The specific school processes are available in this folder, and it is appreciated that this remains consistent with all teachers in the classroom. Class roles and responsibilities are on the task chart on the right side of the main whiteboard in the classroom with short descriptions of each role. These are changed each Friday afternoon. If you are taking my class on a Friday, please don't change the jobs – students know we will catch up on Monday morning.

The teacher next door is Mrs Black, and she has exceptional knowledge of the school. If you need assistance, please see her or the class supervisor, Mr Turner. Thank you for taking the time to support the class today in my absence.

Regards, Mrs West

Leaving 'set' work

If your absence from the class is planned, such as a medical appointment or a day of professional learning, then I recommend leaving a schedule for the day as well as any set learning you feel the class can successfully continue with. Sometimes this is hard to do, as you will likely have a unit of work in motion that you would prefer to implement and observe yourself to ensure progress occurs as planned. Sometimes the unit might be at a place where the students can continue with the relief teacher, but you'll need to leave clear instructions. This does not necessarily mean a whole step-by-step overview with a script – the relief teacher is a still a qualified teacher capable of interpreting curriculum and learning intentions.

I still maintain a short and sweet approach to communicating with the relief teacher – they have a lot of information to absorb in a short amount of time when coming to a new class. It's still a lot of information even if they have had that class before. As I said earlier, no two days are the same for any teacher. So, the overview template and example provided opposite are intended to be kept to one page – typing it out is the best alternative to my messy and rushed handwriting from the day before I'm away from class. If I have any kind of support in my class, such as a learning support officer or support teacher, then I will also email them a copy of the schedule for the day, so they can be aware of any changes and if they need anything for students they might be working with. Even when organisation is well-prepared, I find that open communication is a vital part of ensuring the day is successful for the relief teacher and the students.

This document is also helpful when communicating specific information about class procedures or transitions that may occur during the day. For example, packing away large resources or moving from the classroom to the library. These parts of the schedule may be completely unknown to the relief teacher and it's helpful to allow additional time to maintain calm with the class. It's also helpful to know if the library is a bit of a walk from the classroom and needs to allow time for this transition to occur.

As mentioned, I prefer to type and print this to accompany the relief teacher folder. The support class may be the neighbour teacher or perhaps your supervisor teacher's class. This could also be emailed beforehand if you have contact with the allocated relief teacher or to your supervisor/relief coordinator to ensure it is communicated.

Daily schedule template

Daily Schedule

Casual teacher: (Relief name)	Replacing: (Teacher name)	Class: (name)	Date: ??/??/??

8:30–8:55am	Before school – please check noticeboard in staffroom for changes
9–10:05am **First session**	
10:05–10:15am	Fruit break & brain break
10:15–11:20am **Second session**	
11:20–12:10pm	Lunch & first play break
12:10–1:40pm **Midday session**	
1:40–2pm	Recess & second play break
2–3pm **Afternoon session**	

Support class:	Executive support:

Thank you for taking the class today.

(Insert any additional information here as needed)

Thanks! ☺

Teacher feedback sheet template

Feedback

Casual teacher:	Class:	Date:
Morning session:		
Middle session:		
Afternoon session:		
Message:		
Students highlighted for following expectations:	Concerns to follow up:	

The teacher feedback sheet is intended to be completed by the relief teacher as a way of communication with the class teacher for any follow-up that may need to occur (academic or behavioural).

Individualised feedback sheet template

Individualised Feedback

Student name	Communication

This template could be positive communication or if situations require follow-up with students from the class teacher. Anything serious should be brought to the class supervisor on the day.

Classroom/student preparations

Continuing with the scenario that you know in advance that you will be absent from your class, the classroom itself can be prepped to support the relief teacher and your class. This includes any resources that might be difficult to find or are usually stored in a secure place, such as a locked cabinet or storeroom. Many relief teachers will feel uncomfortable rummaging around a classroom to try and find the correct materials for fear of using something that is personally owned by the class teacher or because they are unsure of the school processes involved in using certain materials. If you want something specific used, leave it in an easily accessible place in the classroom with a clear label for its intended lesson and use, making sure your written plan for the day includes this information.

If you would like to leave school awards, stickers, stamps, etc for the relief teacher to use, also leave these in an accessible place with a clear label with permission to use. If your school policy is that relief teachers are not to use school awards, please make that clear in your introduction letter or organisation for the day. Relief teachers are just as passionate about providing positive experiences for your students, but some schools can have very stringent guidelines, so it's exceptionally helpful if you can guide them to what is appropriate in your school. Many relief teachers will have their own rewards for the day if nothing is available within the classroom.

You can prepare your class in communication throughout the lead-up to the day you will be away. This is useful even if you will still be on school grounds that day (perhaps in professional learning on-site). This may not need to be as stringent as the year goes on and your class becomes accustomed to days when you are absent. Some students may become anxious about the absence, so I recommend enlisting the expertise of your supervisor or learning support team to assist in creating processes to support those student needs. This may also require communicating with those students' parents, so they can also include the changes of routine in their communication and support with their children. Clear communication will yield greater success than not doing so.

Leaving 'general' work

Whether your absence from the class is planned or unplanned, there are potential ways to leave more generalised options for the relief teacher. Your relief teacher folder can contain your overall class schedule for the week, which should entail allocations for subject areas, relief from class, sport, assembly, scripture, etc. This will ensure those learning allocations are still met as much as possible. If your class timetable does not list any support allocations or times when students are withdrawn from your class, then I encourage you to have that documented in addition to your class timetable.

When leaving options for general work, it can still be linked to the curriculum, but in a more open-ended capacity. This could include tasks that are easily adapted to various subject areas and even easily modified for different grades. One example of this could be where students are to create an infographic. This could be digitally or more of a hand-drawn poster style if devices aren't available. The relief teacher can determine if the class works in pairs or small groups. The task can be applied to almost any topic being studied at the time and the class teacher just needs to give some context.

For example:

> This term the class is studying natural and built environments. Our focus has been to compare the school buildings and local community homes and shops to the local playground, parks and natural hiking trails. Students are to complete an infographic of their choice related to any of these concepts. Brainstorm some ideas with the class. Examples can include: 'Dangers to the hiking trails', 'How playgrounds impact local wildlife' or 'Sharing spaces in our community'.

Sometimes it can feel like lazy work to be leaving something more generalised. There is nothing to be ashamed of when leaving tasks that you believe are best suited to your class at the time and space in which this occurs. Not all classes handle change well and sometimes leaving work is a very hard judgement call, even when the class has been prepared for a new face in their classroom.

Examples of general work

Lower primary grades (K–2)	Upper primary grades (3–6)
• New book cover/poster • Think, Pair, Share • Draw, Talk, Write, Share • All about me (drawing, labels, descriptive writing, etc) • Sketch and describe what you see, hear or feel (using an indoor/outdoor space in the classroom or the school)	• New book jacket • Creative alternate ending to something (such as a story, historical event, experiment) • Interview a classmate • Letter to the school principal/teacher • Comic strip design • Create a class quiz

These activities can be modified to suit a particular grade or subject content. For example, in the suggestions above for the upper primary grades I listed 'Create a class quiz'. This could be for any of the content in units being studied in the class that term. It could be history, science or health. Or if it is early in the term, the students could use the content studied the term before. Or it could even be away from the class study focus and be about something the class is interested in, such as movies, TV, music, etc. This activity might appear simple and not really linked to explicit learning, but the activity covers many skills that students are learning. Writing the questions uses handwriting skills, spelling, grammar and punctuation. They need to recall or research the content to also know and record the answer. If working in pairs or small groups, they are practising social skills, such as turn taking and cooperation. Then, of course, they need to use public speaking skills when reading out the questions to the class during the actual quiz. If they record the scores, will they create a scoring chart? Links to mathematics!

Splitting a class

There may be times when the relief teacher is needed for multiple classes across the day, or possibly unavailable at the last minute. This does not mean your class needs aren't important or a priority, sometimes it just means there is a class with different needs. There may be times when this happens at the last minute and it's just unavoidable. As I write this tip, there is a significant teacher shortage across the country (even across the world) and I don't think that will change any time soon. It is very likely that your class will need to be split across other classes at some point in the school year, if not multiple times.

Earlier in this tip I mentioned having a class profile prepared for the relief teacher. I also recommend including a split class list (example over the page). This is a list that identifies which class is best to send students to during this time. This is something that should be discussed with your supervisor, any executive that coordinates teacher absences, your teaching team and any teachers that will be hosting your students when they are split into their classes.

The decision for where students go and who they go with may depend on their relationship with their peers and how they respond to other teachers. If a student does not respond well to a particular teacher, they are likely not going to forge a magical bond on a day that skews the planned routine. It is best to select teachers they know and respond well to. It is appropriate to match up pairs or small groups of students together with others that they work well with and can be trusted to be a support to one another if needed.

For a class split, I recommend having a booklet of work appropriate to the studies being conducted that term. English could include standards skills such as spelling and handwriting. Mathematics could include numeracy such as addition, subtraction, multiplication and division. These booklets should be at a level where students can work independently and ensure students that require modified work have a modified booklet prepared for them. If allowed, have booklets printed so they are ready when needed.

When students are split, consistency helps reduce student anxiety.

Split class list – example

Split List

Student	4A	4B	4/5C	5A	5B	Notes
Katie	X					
Lucas	X					Separate from Daniel
Teddy		X				
Sebastian		X				
Daniel			X			Separate from Lucas
Arabella					X	
Evie					X	
Matthew			X			
Ellie				X		Partial attendance till 12pm
Leon					X	
James					X	
Molly			X			Take ramp desk
Benjamin				X		
Harrison				X		
Millie		X				Stay with Mia
Charlotte	X					
Violet			X			
Robyn			X			
Julia			X			
Charlie				X		
Lilly				X		
Mia		X				Stay with Millie
Lucy	X					
Noah					X	Take extension folder
Amelia					X	
Belle	X					
James		X				Take communication chart
Adam	X					

If any of these classes listed above are not able to take students, please send to 3A or 6B. Please do not send students to 3B or 6A. Please note any changes made to this list and send a copy to the front office, noting any students that are absent.

Be a proactive neighbour teacher

Support your neighbour teacher and their students on days when the teacher is absent. If you know they will be away, have a chat in the lead-up and ask if there is anything you should be aware of before the day. There might be a student with high needs who will be best supported by working in your class for the day, as a familiar face is what will best support them at that time. If your neighbour teacher is absent unexpectedly, I recommend touching base with the relief teacher coordinator and ask if there are any changes you need to be aware of. Pop your head into the classroom and say hello to the relief teacher. Let them know who you are, and you can pass on any pertinent information you feel they need for the day. Schools are very busy and complex places – every little bit we do to help each other creates a positive culture and supports the students dealing with a change to the day.

Tip 9 summary

- Relief teaching has many challenges and complexities, and our students are best supported when we welcome the relief teacher and offer support as best we can.

- Provide clear class information in an overview with a welcome letter and timetable information for the day.

- If your absence is planned, prepare work as you deem appropriate and ensure that all necessary materials and resources for the day are accessible and clearly labelled.

- Having consistent routines and well-maintained organisation in the classroom will support students and the relief teacher during unexpected absences, as the students will know the class expectations for the classroom and their engagement in learning.

- Information for a relief teacher does not need to be scripted; they are professionals, so provide the schedules, overviews and your expectations, and they will manage.

- Prepare ahead of time for the situation that a relief teacher is not available. We have a teacher shortage.

Tip 10

Try an additional role

There will be additional roles within the school to ensure processes and projects are organised. This can be in various formats and may include structured teams or committees. While these groups or teams might run very differently to each other, they are often a great opportunity to collaborate, be innovative and create great opportunities for students, teachers and the school community. For those interested in leadership development in their career, experience in additional roles is a prime opportunity to develop necessary skills and find your potential within the school.

This is also a potential opportunity to share your personal knowledge and experience with your colleagues. You may have been a carpenter before becoming a teacher, perhaps a musician all your life or a dancer. All these skills are not lost because you now call yourself a teacher, and they are skills that are an asset to the school and students across the school – even students that aren't in your class. The teacher who knows how to play an instrument – what an asset for the choir! The teacher who has won awards for their lamingtons – what a life skill to share! Mmm, lamingtons...

I implore with all teachers to identify if they feel comfortable in sharing these skill sets with their school. It's like striking gold to have a teacher share their personal passions and gifts. It doesn't mean you should take on a massive workload to do this, but if you can contribute, I feel it's beneficial to do so. You might not feel ready in your first year of teaching, perhaps you want to test the waters with your own class first and see if you enjoy sharing your personal interests and skills. I love having kids learn from gardening. Now, I don't have the best green thumb but I enjoy it, and it's a great way to model lifelong learning alongside students who garden.

As a team member

For the purposes of this section, I am referring to being a team member in the context of your teaching team. For example, if you are in the mathematics faculty, or the Year 1 teaching team, or in small schools, you might be in the infants team.

Within your teaching team there will come times when various roles and responsibilities are shared similarly and other times when the team will choose to allocate roles and responsibilities based on need, interest or experience. For example, in a Year 6 teaching team there are many events and paperwork that needs to be organised for preparing students to transition to high school. If it is a teacher's first year, then it would be highly difficult for that teacher to have the knowledge and experience required to coordinate everything. So instead, the team might allocate someone with more experience to coordinate the high school enrolment applications, transition days and handover paperwork, while the teacher with less experience could take on the role of coordinating fundraising for the Year 6 Farewell. The workload seems unequal, but it needs to consider everything that needs to be done and might balance out in other areas of responsibilities.

During the organisation of these roles and responsibilities, it is welcome for newly graduated teachers to offer to take on some of these tasks – but be mindful of taking on too much. Remember that your team is likely looking out for your interests in your first year and are there to support you.

As a committee member

Being a committee member is very similar to working with your regular team except you will likely have a main focus area, such as the curriculum, extracurricular activities, school events or a school initiative. Committees also share roles and responsibilities, which may vary depending on experience, interests or workload. Being part of a committee is an opportunity to learn something new or bring an alternative perspective to the team. Communication and organisation will form a significant part of your participation in a committee, so be prepared to listen and contribute professionally.

School projects/initiatives

School projects or initiatives can stem from an identified need within the school and may not always be linked to the curriculum. These projects will likely be identified in school plans and have targets to be achieved within a set time frame. They can be short-term goals or long-term goals. Sometimes the project will have plans to grow, or they may evolve naturally over time. If you are working within one of these projects, it is important to know why the project/initiative was instigated, the goals attached and if there is a roadmap for success included in the planning. Note down if funds are attached to the project/initiative and if there is an estimate of additional time available to complete the work. A common project/initiative example is improving attendance in the school.

Extracurricular activities

In Tip 5, I list many various types of extracurricular activities. I used to dislike the way these activities were described, 'extracurricular', as if they weren't as important as the things learned in the classroom. Now I like it and I believe that this name is because they are extra special. These are the experiences you can't get from a classroom. It takes kids out of their daily environment and gives them a place to express themselves based on their personal passions and interests. This is a time they can be a version of themselves they may not always feel confident to show, and teachers can express themselves in these opportunities as well.

It could be musical, sport, gaming, creating or designing, but it doesn't matter what the actual activity is – the most important part is that the students choose to be there. They are drawn to something that makes them willing to part from friends and precious playtime to be part of something that they love.

Taking part in coordinating an extracurricular activity at some point in your career will give you opportunities to broaden your horizons across the school. It helps to develop great organisational skills, make connections with students outside your class and teaching team, and helps give you a wider perspective of the community in which you teach.

Choosing an activity

As mentioned in Tip 5, there are a wide range of activities that create additional roles within a school. These are usually voluntary, but some schools do have a requirement that all teachers contribute in some way that is not part of your main role as a class teacher. For this to be a successful practice for both you and the students involved, I believe it is important to choose things that align with your interests or your values.

Some activities are based on interests and increasing engagement for students. Others could be to create opportunities for students that aren't available in their local community. Some are competition-based. An example of these differences could be comparing competition sports teams and a knitting group. Sometimes the difference in activity types can impact how much time and effort is required to organise the activity and ensure students all have the best opportunities to connect.

If you don't personally believe in competition-based activities, then I recommend steering clear of those choices (unless of course you wish to give it a try). It is important that you don't compromise your values when you are a significant role model for your students. Never be shy to suggest a new type of activity.

Organisation

In Tip 5, I provided some examples of ways you can coordinate your priorities. On top of this, you will need to ensure your class work and additional work is organised in a timely manner. When taking on an additional role or responsibility, it will be within your scope to determine if it means reducing something in your professional sphere, or if the time will be outside that scope. If you are taking on a load that you believe will require significant amounts of time, it is important to communicate this with your supervisor and ask if there will be any time or supports provided to enable you to do the best job you possibly can. This links in with your workload, and it is important to begin your career with a workload that is sustainable and manageable. If the role you are taking on grows over time, then it might need to evolve into a team-based structure.

Sharing success

Additional roles and activities should be celebrated as much as any classroom success with students, teachers, parents and the community. Especially when it creates opportunities for people to connect, engage and thrive. It doesn't necessarily need to be a large-scale celebration, but consistent methods of communication will help embed pride for the students taking part and recognising the effort and impact of the teacher involved.

Some methods include:

- School newsletter/website/social media
- Celebration boards, for example, for photos
- Displays for awards or final products, for example, Lego creations
- Sharing with local politicians/businesses/school partnerships

Tip 10 summary

- Trying an additional role provides many opportunities to broaden your horizons, meet new people, develop organisational skill sets and contribute to the engagement and connection of students and teachers in the school.

- Being a team member or committee member requires taking on allocated roles and responsibilities where it is important to be mindful of how you contribute and share within the team.

- Some school projects/initiatives might have set requirements and goals to achieve, so it is important to be clear on these expectations before taking it on.

- Extracurricular activities are varied and need different approaches in organisation and implementation. It is a wonderful opportunity to bring your own interests and passions to the school and make others feel welcome.

- Choosing an activity or role to take on should not feel like a burden, but a way to expand. Choose wisely.

- Be organised, plan ahead, prioritise.

- Share successes regularly. Student and teacher success.

Conclusion

It's an evolving career

Being a teacher has been one of the best and unexpected changes in my life. In the later years of high school, I was all set to be a lawyer and life just worked out differently. And I'm grateful for it. I can't imagine any other job where I get to sing, dance, play, experiment, write, paint, run, garden and innovate daily. The role of a teacher has evolved so much from the day I stood in front of my first chalkboard and wrote my name for the class. Just like in the movies. The fact that teaching continues to change with the times is challenging some days, but other days it's what makes our job amazing. No two days are the same, and I love that.

You will have hard days for sure – even experienced teachers do. What you need to remember is that you are not alone. This is not a solitary career; however, you can isolate yourself inadvertently if you don't seek support or work collaboratively when you need to. As a new staff member, it's hard to build relationships with the students, staff and parents, so take it one day at a time. Start with your class, your team and your supervisor, and branch out as you feel comfortable. Try new things and only volunteer for roles when you feel ready to or when you know you will be supported.

A quality teacher cannot burn the candle at both ends. Take care of yourself and keep yourself mentally and physically able to be the amazing teacher you can be. I hope this book helps get you off to a great start as a new teacher. Welcome to teaching!

> "The goal is not to be perfect by the end.
> The goal is to be better tomorrow".
>
> – Simon Sinek

Templates
Sharing is caring

On the following pages, you will access all the templates provided in this book. These include the following:

Tip 3:

- Class Profile Overview template — 121
- Class Profile Overview – example — 122
- Individual Education Plan template — 123
- Individual Education Plan – example — 124
- Weekly timetable template — 127
- Weekly timetable in progress – example — 127
- Timetable in a daybook format – example — 128
- Assessment Schedule template — 129
- Assessment Schedule – example — 132
- Standard 1: Know students and how they learn — 133
- Standard 2: Know the content and how to teach it — 133
- Standard 3: Plan for and implement effective teaching and learning — 134
- Standard 4: Create and maintain supportive and safe learning environments — 134
- Standard 5: Assess, provide feedback and report on student learning — 135

- Standard 6: Engage in professional learning — 135
- Standard 7: Engage professionally with colleagues, parents/carers and the community — 136

Tip 4:
- Relief teacher template — 137
- Completed relief teacher – example — 138
- Report timeline – example — 139

Tip 5:
- Priorities shift template — 140

Tip 9:
- Class letter – example — 141
- Daily schedule template — 142
- Teacher feedback sheet template — 143
- Individualised feedback sheet template — 144
- Split class list – example — 145

Use the QR code to access your own editable copy of the templates provided in the text.

These templates are not for re-sale and may not be reproduced or transmitted in any form or by any means, in whole or part, without the express prior written permission of the author.

Class Profile Overview template

Year: **Grade:**   **Class:**   **Teacher:**

#	Name	Birthday	Age this year	House	Permission to publish	Medical	EALD	PLP	IEP	Glasses	Notes
1											
2											
3											
4											
5											
6											
7											
8											
9											
10											
11											
12											
13											
14											
15											
16											
17											
18											
19											
20											
21											
22											
23											
24											
25											
26											
27											
28											
29											
30											
31											

Key   House groups: Medical: EALD: IEP:

Class Profile Overview – example

Year: 2023 | **Grade:** 2 | **Class:** 2W | **Teacher:** Mrs West

#	Name	Birthday	Age this year	House	Permission to publish	Medical	EALD	PLP	IEP	Glasses	Notes
1	Liam	14/6/2016	7	R	Y			Y			
2	Oliver	20/9/2015	8	R	Y		Vietnamese				
3	Noel	1/6/2016	7	B	Y	Asthma					
4	Elijah	6/2/2016	7	Y	Y		Mandarin TN		Y ASD	Y	Out of Home Care (OOHC)
5	Susan	3/8/2015	8	R	Y						
6	Kate	2/11/2015	8	Y	N			Y			
7	Heidi	6/7/2016	8	Y	Y			Y		Y	
8	Lauren	13/2/2016	7	Y	Y	Asthma					
9	John	25/9/2015	8	R	Y		Vietnamese				New arrival
10	Adam	22/3/2016	7	G	Y				Y Sp		
11	Logan	1/6/2016	7	G	Y						
12	Xavier	7/3/2016	7	G	Y	Diabetes 2					
13	Kathleen	5/2/2016	7	B	Y						Attends OOSH after school
14	Betty	16/7/2015	8	B	Y						
15	Lillian	28/9/2015	8	R	Y		Arabic TN				
16	Esther	30/12/2015	8	G	Y	ANA: eggs			Y ADHD		
17	Alison	31/4/2016	7	Y	N					Y	
18	Lyndall	12/2/2016	7	R	Y		Vietnamese				
19	Ly	1/6/2016	7	G	Y						
20	Stephen	4/3/2016	7	G	Y						
21	Dean	8/8/2015	8	B	Y	ANA: nuts					
22	Nathan	4/10/2015	8	B	Y						
23	Andrew	14/3/2016	7	Y	Y		Samoan TN				
24	Jeffrey	21/10/2015	8	B	N				Y ASD	Y	Court order – Dad no contact
25	Jaye	20/2/2015	8	Y	Y						
26	Kim	2/12/2015	8	Y	Y		Vietnamese				
27	Tara	7/1/2016	7	G	Y	AL: carpet			Y Sp		
28	Cindy	29/7/2015	8	G	Y						
29	Alicia	1/3/2016	7	R	Y		Cantonese				
30	Courtney	6/11/2015	8	B	Y		Arabic	Y			
31	Jackie	3/4/2016	7	G	Y				Y Sp		

Key

House groups: R = Royal, B = Bogus, G = Gang, Y = Yolo

Medical: ANA = anaphylaxis, ALL = allergy

EALD: TN = translator needed for parent communication

IEP: ASD = autism spectrum disorder, Sp = speech diagnosis, ADHD = attention deficit hyperactivity disorder

Individual Education Plan template

Name:	DOB:	Grade/class:	Teacher:	IEP start date:	IEP review dates:
Diagnosis/disability confirmation		Funding	School support		External support

Student strengths	Student interests

Student goals	Parent goals	Teacher goals

Additional information:

SMART GOALS – Specific, Measurable, Actionable, Relevant, Timely

Focus area	SMART goal	Strategies/adjustments	Responsibility	Monitoring

Review meetings

Date/time/staff	Review and evaluation of goals	Further action

Sharing is caring

Individual Education Plan – example

Name: Elijah Johns	DOB: 6/3/2016	Grade/class: Year 1, 1/2W	Teacher: Rebecca West	IEP start date: 28/2/2022	IEP review dates: Term 1, Week 10
Diagnosis/disability confirmation		Funding		School support	External support
Autism spectrum disorder		$8,043 (integration funding support)		LST, SLSO class support	NDIS – speech + occupational therapy

Student strengths

Student strengths	Student interests
Friendly and kind	Computers and computer games
Very positive attitude to school and learning	Trains (and various other transport)
Extremely creative with computer games and computers in general	Painting and drawing
Very good at reading	Spending time with family

Student goals	Parent goals	Teacher goals
To read harder books	Develop strong friendships	Comprehension skills – inferential specifically
To get better at handwriting	Build resilience when he fails/loses at something	Improve confidence in trying new things
Make more friends	Improve fine motor skills – writing/cutting	Improve fine motor skills
Get faster at running	Comprehension skills	Support development of friendships

Additional information:
Elijah has many friends at school and is well-liked by his peers. He seems to often spend his playtime with students in younger grades as he has found it difficult to manage challenging moments with children his own age. Elijah struggles to articulate his feelings when he is not managing a situation and finds this frustrating, so he enjoys playing with younger students as he does not encounter this issue as much with younger peers. Elijah gets along very well with peers in class time and enjoys participating in activities and discussions where teacher support enables a positive level of interaction with his peers. Sometimes Elijah finds the thought of failing or losing more challenging than when it actually happens, and this sometimes impacts his willingness to play with peers his own age.

124 Talkin' Chalk

SMART GOALS – Specific, Measurable, Actionable, Relevant, Timely

Focus area	SMART goal	Strategies/adjustments	Responsibility	Monitoring
Goal 1: Literacy – comprehension	By the end of Week 8, Term 2, Elijah will be able to read and comprehend a level 8 decodable text.	Elijah will participate in guided reading sessions four times per week with the class teacher. He will receive familiar reading sessions two times per week with an SLSO. He will receive allocated support time during literacy sessions to support comprehension tasks based on modelled and guided reading sessions over the term. Parents have agreed to read decodable texts with Elijah at home for at least 20 minutes per day and engage in asking questions and discuss the text.	Class teacher SLSO (parents)	Elijah will be monitored through ongoing observations by the class teacher and SLSO. Parents will submit reading logs weekly with homework. He will be assessed on reading fluency and comprehension using the Sparkle Kit.
Goal 2: Literacy – fine motor	By the end of Week 9, Term 1, Elijah will be able to independently trace over shapes and letters with at least 80% accuracy and write his own name independently.	Elijah will be provided with targeted fine motor tasks during literacy rotations and work 1:1 with the SLSO. Tasks will be based on fine motor skills that support hand development such as cutting, squishing, pinching, etc, as guided by his occupational therapist (example tasks in files). The SLSO will only use the hand-over-hand technique when providing explicit teaching strategies. Elijah will practise writing his name every day and be given tracing tasks within his homework in lieu of sentence writing. Parents have agreed to this substitute to prioritise fine motor development for this term.	Class teacher SLSO (parents)	Elijah will be monitored by collecting work samples regularly and monitoring the transference of skills to handwriting and writing sessions in class.
Goal 3: Social emotional – friendships	By the end of Week 9, Term 1, Elijah will learn key phrases to join games with peers near to his own age and apply these in both class and playground situations.	Elijah will participate in the social skills group program coordinated by the school psychologist. The program will run once a week for one hour with a small group of students near to Elijah's own age. Students will develop friendship skills related to the classroom and the playground. The class teacher and SLSO will receive resources and feedback from the school psychologist to ensure consistency of language and skill development throughout the program. The school psychologist and SLSO will also monitor for developments in the playground (timetable to be rescheduled).	School psychologist Class teacher SLSO	Elijah will be monitored through the social skills program, classroom/playground observations and monitoring any records of incidents with other students. Elijah will have the opportunity to self-reflect during the social skills program. Parents will be asked of any change in situations outside school, for example, local park.
Goal 4: Social emotional – resilience	By the end of Week 8, Term 2, Elijah will be able to choose a learned technique when finding it difficult to remain calm during a situation related to loss or failure.	Elijah will participate in the class Welcome Circle and Smiling Minds, which the teacher will specifically design around resilience. The whole class will participate in sessions to learn about growth mindset and resilience. The teacher/SLSO will work in small groups where Elijah can participate with peers of his choosing that he feels safe with to engage in targeted activities that model breathing techniques, walk-away techniques and using key phrases to help calm down. The teacher will install an 'emotional thermometer' in the classroom and incorporate this resource into the school PBL lessons. The teacher will create anchor charts for the class and provide mini versions for Elijah's desk to support him in using techniques during challenging situations. The school psychologist will also use the same resources in their sessions during the social skills program.	Class teacher SLSO support School psychologist support	The teacher will monitor Elijah's development against previous records where checklists were used to record the regularity of incidents where Elijah did not participate due to fear of failure or had difficulty calming down. Teacher and SLSO will observe the use of techniques learned during class sessions and Elijah will be asked to self-reflect on how he feels when using the breathing or calming techniques.

SMART GOALS – Specific, Measurable, Actionable, Relevant, Timely continued...

Date/time/staff	Review meetings	
	Review and evaluation of goals	Further action
Term 1, Week 10 Tuesday Class teacher, SLSO, school psychologist, learning and support teacher, parents	**Goal 1: Literacy – comprehension.** Elijah can successfully read and comprehend a level 7 decodable text. **Goal 2: Literacy – fine motor.** Elijah can independently write his own name and trace over letters and shapes with 80% accuracy. **Goal 3: Social emotional – friendships.** Elijah has been able to use some of the strategies learned during the social skills group in the classroom setting and in the playground. He still needs some guidance and support from the teacher or from other peers who feel more confident using the strategies. **Goal 4: Social emotional – resilience.** Elijah has found it difficult to respond to the use of breathing techniques and says he finds it hard to focus on breathing when he is feeling overwhelmed. He has said he thinks everyone is looking at him when he is trying to calm down and would prefer to be alone and walk away. Elijah said he likes the emotional thermometer and the anchor charts on his desk.	**Goal 1:** Elijah will continue with guided reading groups, familiar reading and home reading next term. **Goal 2:** Elijah will continue this process with small words and drawings using shapes. **Goal 3:** Elijah will continue with the social skills program for five more weeks next term with some new students included in the program to support him transitioning these skills with new people. Parents report he has only tried these skills twice outside the school context, once was with family. **Goal 4:** Teacher will trial the use of a calm down space in the classroom of Elijah's choosing and print out the emotional thermometer and anchor charts to be placed in the calm down space. Teacher will create a flowchart with Elijah about the steps and expectations for using this space to calm down in difficult scenarios. School psychologist will also identify a place in the playground that is safe and appropriate for Elijah to calm down during playtime and print out the above resources to be placed in a playground location to support Elijah using these strategies.

Weekly timetable template

	Mon	Tue	Wed	Thu	Fri
8:30–9am					
9–10am					
10–11am					
11–11:20am					
11:20–12:10pm	Lunch	Lunch	Lunch	Lunch	Lunch
12:10–1:10pm					
1:10–1:40pm					
1:40–2pm	Recess	Recess	Recess	Recess	Recess
2–3pm					
Meetings					
Notes					

Weekly timetable in progress – example

	Mon	Tue	Wed	Thu	Fri
8:30–9am		Admin meeting			
9–10am	Class roll Reading Spelling	Class roll Reading News groups	Class roll Library	Class roll Scripture Writing	Class roll Reading Spelling
10–11am	Fruit break Writing	Fruit break Writing	Fruit break Spelling	Fruit break Reading	Fruit break Health
11–11:20am	Handwriting	~~Buddy reading~~	Grammar	Fitness	Handwriting
11:20–12:10pm	Lunch	Lunch	Lunch	Lunch	Lunch
12:10–1:10pm	Maths	Maths	Maths	Maths	Sport
1:10–1:40pm	Science	Maths	Creative arts	Health	Sport
1:40–2pm	Recess	Recess	Recess	Recess	Recess
2–3pm	Science	Fitness	Creative arts	HSIE	Assembly
Meetings			STAFF PL – maths		
Notes	Ran out of time for handwriting	Buddy reading cancelled as teacher was sick			

Sharing is caring

Timetable in a daybook format – example

	Monday	To-do	Notes
8:30–9am		Laminate name tags	Ran out of time for handwriting
9–10am	Class roll Reading – Matilda, Chapter 4 Spelling – 'ai'	Submit PL application	
10–11am	Fruit break Writing – comic strips	Complete maths program for Week 7	
11–11:20am	Handwriting – clockwise letters	LST meeting follow-up with counsellor	
11:20–12:10pm	Lunch		
12:10–1:10pm	Maths – fractions		
1:10–1:40pm	Science – STEM lab with Mr T – Volcano!		
1:40–2pm	Recess		
2–3pm	Science – STEM lab with Mr T – Volcano!		
Meetings			

Assessment Schedule template

School name – Year Assessment Schedule

Term	Wk	Kindergarten	Stage 1	Stage 2	Stage 3	Notes
1	1					
	2					
	3					
	4					
	5					
	6					
	7					
	8					
	9					
	10					
2	1					
	2					
	3					
	4					
	5					
	6					
	7					
	8					
	9					
	10					

Assessment Schedule template

School name – Year Assessment Schedule

Term	Wk	Kindergarten	Stage 1	Stage 2	Stage 3	Notes
3	1					
	2					
	3					
	4					
	5					
	6					
	7					
	8					
	9					
	10					
4	1					
	2					
	3					
	4					
	5					
	6					
	7					
	8					
	9					
	10					

Assessment Schedule template

Name	Notes										As-needed assessments								
	Details, links etc.										*Details, links etc.*								
Name											**Name**								

Assessment schedule – example

Term	Wk	Kindergarten	Stage 1	Stage 2	Stage 3
1	1	Best Start Formal	AWESOME TEST		
	2		SENA	SENA	SENA
	3		SA Spelling	SA Spelling	SA Spelling
	4		Reading + comprehension	Reading + comprehension	Reading + comprehension
	5	Intervention Graphs	Intervention Graphs + PLAN 2	Intervention Graphs + PLAN 2	Intervention Graphs + PLAN 2
	6	Writing sample	Writing sample	Writing sample	Writing sample
	7	TEN	TEN	PAT-M	PAT-M
	8	Reading + PLAN 2	Reading + PLAN 2	Reading + PLAN 2	Reading + PLAN 2
	9	CTJ + Intervention Graphs/data	CTJ + Intervention Graphs/data	CTJ + Intervention Graphs/data	CTJ + Intervention Graphs/data
	10	Planning day	Planning day	Planning day	Planning day
2	1				
	2	Writing sample	Writing sample	Writing sample	Writing sample
	3	TEN	TEN/Maths diagnostic	Reading + comprehension	Reading + comprehension
	4	Reading	Reading + comprehension	NAPLAN	NAPLAN
	5	Intervention Graphs + PLAN 2	Intervention Graphs + PLAN 2	Intervention Graphs + PLAN 2	Intervention Graphs + PLAN 2
	6			Maths diagnostic	Maths diagnostic
	7	Reports to supervisors	Reports to supervisors	Reports to supervisors	Reports to supervisors
	8	Reading + PLAN 2	Reading + PLAN 2	Reading + PLAN 2	Reading + PLAN 2
	9	CTJ + Intervention Graphs/data	CTJ + Intervention Graphs/data	CTJ + Intervention Graphs/data	CTJ + Intervention Graphs/data
	10	Planning day	Planning day	Planning day	Planning day

Notes

Intervention Graphs	Identify tier 1, 2 and 3 students (including extension) in the intervention chart with blue, green, yellow and red sections. Students listed as yellow on intervention graphs are prime subjects for PLAN 2 monitoring. Yellow students to have work samples and personalised learning goals on data wall – created and updated with it.
CTJ	Consistent Teacher Judgement – complete formative/summative assessment and analyse across the team. Update personalised learning goals during team planning with AP and IL.
PLAN 2	Review student data and update tracking on PLAN 2. Discuss changes to intervention graphs with AP/IL and update personalised learning goals on data wall.
TEN/PAT-M/diagnostic	Use the listed assessment tool for all students. Analyse data, collect work samples and create personalised numeracy goals with it.
Writing	Cold writing sample using a stimulus for whole class and assess against rubric. Shared marking between the grade/stage. Create personalised writing goals on data wall.
Reading/comp	PM reading level tracking (Kindy to include sounds and vocab assessments). Comprehensive rubric monitored once a term. Collect samples for data wall and creating of reading goals on data wall.
Reports	Academic reports due to supervisors – all grades and comments.

STANDARD 1: Know students and how they learn

Focus area

1.1 Physical, social and intellectual development and characteristics of students
1.2 Understand how students learn
1.3 Students with diverse linguistic, cultural, religious and socioeconomic backgrounds
1.4 Strategies for teaching Aboriginal and Torres Strait Islander students
1.5 Differentiate teaching to meet the specific learning needs of students across the full range of abilities
1.6 Strategies to support full participation of students with disability

Focus area	Artefact 1	Artefact 2	Artefact 3	Artefact 4
1.1				
1.2				
1.3				
1.4				
1.5				
1.6				

STANDARD 2: Know the content and how to teach it

Focus area

2.1 Content and teaching strategies of the teaching area
2.2 Content selection and organisation
2.3 Curriculum, assessment and reporting
2.4 Understand and respect Aboriginal and Torres Strait Islander people to promote reconciliation between Indigenous and non-Indigenous Australians
2.5 Literacy and numeracy strategies
2.6 Information and Communication Technology (ICT)

Focus area	Artefact 1	Artefact 2	Artefact 3	Artefact 4
2.1				
2.2				
2.3				
2.4				
2.5				
2.6				

STANDARD 3: Plan for and implement effective teaching and learning

Focus area

3.1 Establish challenging learning goals
3.2 Plan, structure and sequence learning programs
3.3 Use teaching strategies
3.4 Select and use resources
3.5 Use effective classroom communication
3.6 Evaluate and improve teaching programs
3.7 Engage parents/carers in the educative process

Focus area	Artefact 1	Artefact 2	Artefact 3	Artefact 4
3.1				
3.2				
3.3				
3.4				
3.5				
3.6				
3.7				

STANDARD 4: Create and maintain supportive and safe learning environments

Focus area

4.1 Support student participation
4.2 Manage classroom activities
4.3 Manage challenging behaviour
4.4 Maintain student safety
4.5 Use ICT safely, responsibly and ethically

Focus area	Artefact 1	Artefact 2	Artefact 3	Artefact 4
4.1				
4.2				
4.3				
4.4				
4.5				

STANDARD 5: Assess, provide feedback and report on student learning

Focus area

5.1 Assess student learning

5.2 Provide feedback to students on their learning

5.3 Make consistent and comparable judgements

5.4 Interpret student data

5.5 Report on student achievement

Focus area	Artefact 1	Artefact 2	Artefact 3	Artefact 4
5.1				
5.2				
5.3				
5.4				
5.5				

STANDARD 6: Engage in professional learning

Focus area

6.1 Identify and plan professional learning needs

6.2 Engage in professional learning and improve practice

6.3 Engage with colleagues and improve practice

6.4 Apply professional learning and improve student learning

Focus area	Artefact 1	Artefact 2	Artefact 3	Artefact 4
6.1				
6.2				
6.3				
6.4				

STANDARD 7: Engage professionally with colleagues, parents/carers and the community

Focus area

7.1 Meet professional ethics and responsibilities

7.2 Comply with legislative, administrative and organisational requirements

7.3 Engage with the parents/carers

7.4 Engage with professional teaching networks and broader communities

Focus area	Artefact 1	Artefact 2	Artefact 3	Artefact 4
7.1				
7.2				
7.3				
7.4				

Relief teacher template

Daily Schedule

| Casual teacher: | Replacing: | Class: | Date: |

8:30–8:55am	Before school – please check noticeboard in staffroom for changes
9–10:15am	**Roll** **First session**
10:15–11:20am	**Fruit break** **Second session**
11:20–12:10pm	Lunch
12:10–1:40pm	**Middle session** **Warm-up game**
Recess	
2–3pm	**Afternoon session**

| Timeout support class: | Executive support: |

Thank you for taking the class today.

Sharing is caring

Completed relief teacher – example

Daily Schedule

Casual teacher: Monika	Replacing: Rebecca	Class: 2 Topaz	Date: 30/8/17

8:30–8:55am	Before school – please check noticeboard in staffroom for changes
9–10:15am	**Roll** – ask students to read their familiar readers (n the red box) for 10 minutes. **Guided reading groups** – activities are at the back cupboard. The students can help put them out on the tables. Students can move around the activities at their own choice, including Google Classroom (only the students who haven't done their D&D character sheet). Please read with Max (on his own) and Oliver and Liam together – if he will read. When finished, please make sure students pack up properly and put resources in the back cupboard neatly.
10:15–11:20am	**Fruit break** – please read a story from the whiteboard while students eat their fruit. **Writing** – join with the class next door for the writing session. The class teacher is expecting you and will have everything. Please support her with the class. Students Isabella, William, Emma and Ben will need the most support.
11:20–12:10pm	Lunch & first play break
12:10–1:40pm	**Maths:** **Warm-up game** – students play 'Addition Wars'. They have played it a few times this week and know how to play. Ask them to show you how to play as practice, then they can get into small groups to play (cards are at the bottom of the whiteboard). **Word problem** – (students will need some support for this) Write the problem on the board and have children identify the important parts and words. *Calvin read his book for 3 minutes every night for a week. Hobbes read his book for 5 minutes every night. How much more time did Hobbes spend reading his book compared to Calvin last week?* Then write this up and go through this – talk about how it is more open-ended. Students can copy this problem into their maths book (with short date and a title): *Calvin read his book for 3 minutes every night for a week. Hobbes read his book for 5 minutes every night.* *The answers are 35, 2, 21, 56, 14. What might the questions be?* **Maths games** – there are maths games in the storeroom on the left on the bottom shelf. Students can play those if there is extra time.
Recess	
2–3pm	**Science** – in the back of Science books (in tray on back shelf), ask students to write their own description for how to make a paper airplane (they followed instructions to make one yesterday). Write up on the whiteboard an example of the steps and include pictures of the paper folding. Ask them how they followed the steps and what made it easy or hard to understand in the instructions they used yesterday. Make sure you remind students to use neat writing and to take care when drawing their pictures.

Timeout support class: *2 Quartz*	Executive support: *Ms Ayad (Principal)*

Thank you for taking the class today. You will see that Max doesn't work independently. The SLSO Maya will come and take him to read, but when he comes in the room you will need to make him sit at an activity and ask a student to help him. (He has activities in his silver folder on his desk but needs help with most of it.) Wei or James work well with him. They are a very fun class that respond best to positive reinforcement, praise and humour. Feel free to give them as many Dojo Points as you like and remind them they have a reward on Friday if they continue doing the right thing.

Thanks! Bec ☺

Report timeline – example

Due dates	Report schedule tasks	My to-do list
Holidays		Effort scores all KLAs
Week 1		Comments for PDHPE, Sci & Tech, CA
Week 2		Maths comments
Week 3		English comments
Monday **Week 4**	Set up Academic Reporting Period online	Proofread all KLAs and edit where needed. Check comments against achievement scores
Monday **Week 6**	Comments and grades to supervisors	Hand into supervisor. Make necessary edits
Monday **Week 8**	Completed reports due to supervisors	
Friday **Week 8**	Attendance data imported onto reports by executive	
Tuesday **Week 9**	Reports printed by admin staff (back-up day Thursday)	Sign reports
Monday **Week 10**	REPORTS GO HOME	Hand out to students. Absent reports to office

Priorities shift template

	Class	Choir	Notes
Week 1		Prep for open day	
Week 2	Open day	Open day	
Week 3			
Week 4	Reading data	No rehearsal	*(or Mrs White run)*
Week 5	Running assembly	Longer rehearsal	
Week 6	Maths data	No rehearsal	*(or Mrs White run)*
Week 7			
Week 8	Reports due		
Week 9		2 rehearsals to prep for performance	*Mrs White to take 2nd rehearsal*
Week 10		Performance	

Class letter – example

Dear relief teacher,

Thank you for taking my class today. You will be provided with an information folder containing organisation for the school and the class, as well as pertinent information about the students. You will notice I have a slightly smaller class, however, some of the students have high complexities requiring additional support. You might have support staff join the class throughout the day. There may be some learning support officers scheduled to come in and support specific student needs and other teachers will join the class to provide general support to the class. If the identified student they work with is absent, they might have another student to work with, or might support the class in general – or they may need to change their schedule and support a student from another class. When additional staff join the class, please clarify with them what their role is in the class so you are aware of what they will be doing when they join the class. We appreciate your flexibility and understanding that the support staff roles and timetable may change during the day if changes occur. If students are required to leave the classroom, such as an intervention program, please ensure they line up at the door when it is time to go with the messenger and remind them of school expectations to walk quietly, safely and respectfully to their session.

Please don't feel it is a requirement to push through all the work for the day. Having a different teacher can sometimes be overwhelming to this class, so please take the time to ensure students are settled and ready to learn for each session. If this means having a long breathing exercise or brain break, I appreciate you taking the additional time to allow students to settle before engaging in the class work. Students will respond positively when they know you allow them the time they need to be mentally and physically prepared to learn.

Our classroom is located near the toilets, which makes it very easy for students to have quick toilet breaks during class time. We also have sinks nearby for refilling water bottles and students are permitted their water bottles on their desk throughout the day. Please don't allow any other drinks inside the classroom space such as milk or juice, as the whole classroom is carpeted. If the day is very hot, the class will sit at their desk to eat lunch, otherwise there are silver seats just outside the classroom door that students will sit at during eating time.

Our class embeds the use of growth mindset and restorative practices. Any kind of rewards incentive used in the class operates separately to any consequences. The specific school processes are available in this folder, and it is appreciated that this remains consistent with all teachers in the classroom. Class roles and responsibilities are on the task chart on the right side of the main whiteboard in the classroom with short descriptions of each role. These are changed each Friday afternoon. If you are taking my class on a Friday, please don't change the jobs – students know we will catch up on Monday morning.

The teacher next door is Mrs Black, and she has exceptional knowledge of the school. If you need assistance, please see her or the class supervisor, Mr Turner. Thank you for taking the time to support the class today in my absence.

Regards, Mrs West

Daily schedule template

Daily Schedule

Casual teacher: *(Relief name)*	Replacing: *(Teacher name)*	Class: *(name)*	Date: ??/??/??

8:30–8:55am	Before school – please check noticeboard in staffroom for changes
9–10:05am **First session**	
10:05–10:15am	Fruit break & brain break
10:15–11:20am **Second session**	
11:20–12:10pm	Lunch & first play break
12:10–1:40pm **Midday session**	
1:40–2pm	Recess & second play break
2–3pm **Afternoon session**	

Support class:	Executive support:

Thank you for taking the class today.

(Insert any additional information here as needed)

Thanks! ☺

Teacher feedback sheet template

Feedback

Casual teacher:		Class:	Date:
Morning session:			
Middle session:			
Afternoon session:			
Message:			
Students highlighted for following expectations:		Concerns to follow up:	

Individualised feedback sheet template

Individualised Feedback

Student name	Communication

Split class list – example

Split List

Student	4A	4B	4/5C	5A	5B	Notes
Katie	X					
Lucas	X					Separate from Daniel
Teddy		X				
Sebastian		X				
Daniel			X			Separate from Lucas
Arabella					X	
Evie					X	
Matthew			X			
Ellie				X		Partial attendance till 12pm
Leon					X	
James					X	
Molly			X			Take ramp desk
Benjamin				X		
Harrison				X		
Millie		X				Stay with Mia
Charlotte	X					
Violet			X			
Robyn			X			
Julia			X			
Charlie				X		
Lilly				X		
Mia		X				Stay with Millie
Lucy	X					
Noah					X	Take extension folder
Amelia					X	
Belle	X					
James			X			Take communication chart
Adam	X					

About the author

Bec West entered her teaching pathway in 1999 when she was accepted into a Bachelor of Education (Primary) degree with the University of Western Sydney – now known as Western Sydney University. It was her safety net course, recommended by her parents, as she was intending to study law. It didn't really matter, though. In her fourth week of the first semester, Bec went to her first practicum, a Kindergarten class in a school in southwest Sydney, and she loved it. Hasn't looked back ever since. She has been teaching since 2003, and also continued to study, gaining a Bachelor of Special Education, a Master of Education and is currently studying a Master of Educational Leadership.

The mother of three children, who are all still school-aged. Bec has gained some valuable insights of what it's like from the parent perspective to engage with schools and manage home life alongside school life. She has been able to learn what school is like through her own children's experiences and reflections. Bec strives to forge positive connections with parents and communities to ensure education is a holistic and connected experience for all.

Bec is an innovative educational leader who has been working in schools for 20 years. She is currently the Foundation Deputy Principal in a new school with previous roles including K-6 classroom teacher, Assistant Principal, Assistant Principal: Curriculum and Instruction, Deputy Principal: Instructional Leader and relieving principal. Passionate about equity, creativity and innovation, she is a proud public educator, lifelong learner and dedicated leader.

Throughout her career, Bec has enjoyed the experiences that working in a school brings, including coordinating choir, dance and student leadership initiatives, sports coaching, leading teaching committees, creating curriculum supports and school fundraising.

In her two decades of teaching, Bec has worked in a variety of settings, including a special education setting, large schools, small schools and a K-12 school; she has enjoyed the experiences of working in both rural country and metropolitan areas. She has high experience in schools with complex enrolments including working with communities with high percentages of English as an Additional Language/Dialect (EAL/D) and Aboriginal and/or Torres Strait Islander students.

Bec has become a strong advocate for inclusive education, future-focused learning and leading positive change. She focuses on fostering collaborative relationships and enhancing education by building the capacity of students, teachers and the community.

Bec is dedicated to facilitating quality professional learning for educators and leaders at any point in their career and has become known for supporting the ongoing development of teachers and students through her YouTube channels Talkin' Chalk and Clever Pickles. Her commitment to education has been recognised as an example of how education can transform young students' lives, especially in disadvantaged communities.

In 2021, Bec was a recipient of the Commonwealth Bank Teaching Awards and became one of 12 Teaching Fellows. She was also listed as a Top 10 Finalist in the 2021 Global Teacher Prize for which she received letters of commendation from local members of parliament and the Prime Minister of Australia. Bec has also received the Director's Award for significant achievement in the role of School Executive.

Bec taught in New South Wales at the beginning of her career and has recently embarked on a new adventure as a Deputy Principal in sunny Queensland. As she says goodbye to the NSW portion of her career, she wants to ensure that new graduates beginning their teaching career are supported with the knowledge and experience she gained in her time there.

www.ingramcontent.com/pod-product-compliance
Lightning Source LLC
Chambersburg PA
CBHW050239120526
44590CB00016B/2147